OUR CHANGING WHITE HOUSE

This book was published in close cooperation with the White House Historical Association and the Office of the Curator, the White House. The work is an outgrowth of the two hundredth anniversary celebration of the laying of the cornerstone for the White House.

OUR CHANGING WHITE HOUSE

Edited by
WENDELL GARRETT

NORTHEASTERN UNIVERSITY PRESS

Boston

Northeastern University Press

Copyright 1995 by The White House Historical Association

The publication of this volume has been supported in part by a
grant from the National Endowment for the Humanities.

Library of Congress Cataloging-in-Publication Data
Our changing White House / edited by Wendell Garrett.
p. cm.
Includes index.
ISBN 1-55553-222-5
1. White House (Washington, D.C.).   2. Washington (D.C.)—
Buildings, structures, etc.   I. Garrett, Wendell D.
F204.W5O98   1995
975.3—dc20   94-43182

Designed by Joyce C. Weston

Composed in Sabon by Wellington Graphics, Westwood,
Massachusetts. Printed and bound by Quebecor/
Kingsport, Kingsport, Tennessee. The paper is
Glatfelter Offset, an acid-free stock.

MANUFACTURED IN THE UNITED STATES OF AMERICA
99 98 97 96 95   5 4 3 2 1

Jacqueline Kennedy's vision for the White House Historical Association, which she created in 1961, was the publication and the dissemination of factual historical and educational material relating to the White House. The Association, which has been faithful to her charge, is pleased to dedicate the second volume of papers presented during the two hundredth anniversary celebration of the White House to the memory of Jacqueline Bouvier Kennedy Onassis as the inspiration for the founding of the White House Historical Association and for the extraordinary contribution she made to the President's House.

CONTENTS

LIST OF CONTRIBUTORS

WILLIAM G. ALLMAN is the Assistant Curator of the White House. He has served in the Office of the Curator, participating in the documentation and interpretation of the history of the White House and the White House collections, since 1976.

BARBARA G. CARSON teaches material culture at both George Washington University and the College of William and Mary and is a consultant at many museums and historic sites. She is the author of *The Governor's Palace: The Williamsburg Residence of Virginia's Royal Governor* and *Ambitious Appetites: Dining, Behavior, and Consumption in Federal Washington.*

MARJORIE HUNT is a folklorist with the Smithsonian Institution's Center for Folklife Programs and Cultural Studies. Her extensive work in occupational culture and oral history includes the Academy Award–winning film *The Stone Carvers* and the video documentary *Workers at the White House.*

WILLIAM KLOSS serves on the Committee for the Preservation of the White House, originally appointed by President Bush and reappointed by President Clinton. He is the author of *Art in the White House: A Nation's Pride, Samuel F. B. Morse,* and *Treasures from the National Museum of American Art,* and a major contributor to *Treasures of State.*

BETTY C. MONKMAN is the Associate Curator at the White House and curator of the first exhibition on the architectural history of the White

House, "The White House 1792–1992: Image in Architecture." She has lectured and written extensively on the history of the White House and its collections.

LEE H. NELSON, FAIA (1928–1994), served for thirty-two years with the National Park Service as a historical architect and administrator in the technical preservation services program. His work on Independence Hall is both nationally and internationally recognized; he most recently served as advisor for the restoration of the exterior stonework of the White House. He created the "Preservation Briefs" series and authored numerous publications, including *White House Stone Carving: Builders and Restorers*.

WILLIAM SEALE is a historian active in the restoration of state capitols and historic houses throughout the United States. He is the author of *The President's House, The White House: The History of an American Idea, Of Houses and Time*, and *Domes of America*.

SUZANNE TURNER is Professor and Graduate Coordinator for the School of Landscape Architecture at Louisiana State University. She also works as a consultant for the preservation, interpretation, and management of historic landscapes. She is the author of numerous articles on landscape preservation and the interpretation of historic landscapes, and the recipient of a summer fellowship at Dumbarton Oaks in 1992.

GARY WALTERS is the Chief Usher of the White House, having served in that capacity since the Reagan administration. He is responsible for the preservation and operation of the Executive Residence and grounds.

RICHARD GUY WILSON is Commonwealth Professor of Architectural History at the University of Virginia. He has written extensively on Thomas Jefferson, McKim, Mead & White, and the American Renaissance, and he has received numerous awards.

FOREWORD

In October of 1992, the White House Historical Association and the National Park Service jointly sponsored a symposium celebrating the two hundredth anniversary of the laying of the cornerstone of the White House. Following that event, Northeastern University Press published an illustrated selection of papers presented by noted participants in the symposium, *The White House: The First Two Hundred Years,* edited by Frank Freidel and William Pencak. Northeastern University Press is now publishing this second, lavishly illustrated compilation of papers largely from the symposium.

Publications such as these are central to the White House Historical Association's mission to instill knowledge and appreciation of the White House and its history. The Association was founded in 1961 in response to Jacqueline Kennedy's desire to maintain and refurbish the White House, and to increase awareness of the White House's past. The Association's first publication was a guidebook created, in the words of Mrs. Kennedy, to help visitors "sort out the impressions received on an often crowded visit." The White House, as she was surely aware, is the most toured historic home in the nation, welcoming more than one million visitors annually. Since that time, more than eight million copies of White House Historical Association books have been sold. The proceeds have gone toward preservation projects in the White House, for the acquisition of fine and decorative arts, and for the production of educational materials about the Executive Mansion.

This volume, *Our Changing White House,* continues in the worthwhile tradition begun so many years ago by Mrs. Kennedy. The papers within reveal a White House forever evolving, evoking our nation's past and shaping its future. This book serves as a tribute to Jacqueline Bouvier Kennedy Onassis, and to all who have strived to preserve and interpret this American landmark.

ROBERT L. BREEDEN
Chair, White House Historical Association

INTRODUCTION

In 1690 the English philosopher John Locke, echoing the familiar words from Genesis, wrote, "In the beginning, all the world was America." Like the Garden of Eden before the Fall, America seemed to Locke and many others in the Old World to stand at the dawn of a new history—radiant with opportunities.

This idea, enduring for centuries, haunted Europeans and Americans alike. "America is opportunity," commented Ralph Waldo Emerson—and how many different kinds of opportunity! "It is hard to resist the temptation to express one's admiration for the richness and variety of the forms in which civilization has developed itself in America, for the inexhaustible inventiveness and tireless energy of the people," opined Lord Bryce in 1905. The White House, the ever-changing home of the president, stands as a testament to the long metamorphosis of the nation it represents.

In the early years of the new republic, rhetoric extolled the nation's guiding principles of liberty, justice, and equality. As these abstractions gained rallying power, they took visible shape in the form of symbols of national unity. The President's House—as the White House was originally known—along with the Capitol, the Declaration of Independence, the Fourth of July, the Constitution, the national flag, the apotheosis of Washington, and the pantheon of Revolutionary War heroes, became a venerable, outward, visible sign of the invisible knitting together of local and regional loyalties into a national heritage and identity.

The District of Columbia, and thus the White House, was located on the Potomac River as a result of a political compromise forged in Congress. The central location of the Potomac, its accessible but defensible position, the closeness of its headwaters to the Ohio River and thereby to a vast area of inland country, and George Washington's sponsorship of the site led to the Residence Act of 1790. The law provided for a ten-year interregnum at Philadelphia while the new capital was being planted in the Potomac wilderness and stipulated that Congress would move the new seat of government in 1800.

Originally ten miles square, the District of Columbia was a diamond set at the head of navigation on the Potomac River with its corners pointed directly north, east, south, and west. Within its proposed boundary were the two extant thriving port cities of Georgetown on the Maryland side of the river and Alexandria on the Virginia side. Pierre-Charles L'Enfant was hired to design the Federal District, and like the constitutional plan for the federal government, his plan was intended to express the separation of powers. The Capitol, the President's House, and the Supreme Court were to be separated by considerable distances and situated to command different aspects. The streets were to radiate in all directions, a symbolic invitation to citizens to come and be heard. George Washington himself devoted an enormous amount of time during the last decade of his life to the federal city, becoming embroiled in many personality clashes and minute details, in addition to choosing designs and architects. The city was named in Washington's honor on September 9, 1791.

Washington's closest advisor in matters relating to the capital city was Thomas Jefferson, and he became the guiding spirit for federal architecture. Jefferson lamented the cultural inexperience of his countrymen, complaining of the absence of "a model among us sufficiently chaste" to elevate the sights of "mostly self-taught designers with a bent for unruly ornamentation." He owned the largest architecture library in the United States, and his personal taste in buildings ran toward the Renaissance classicism of Andrea Palladio. The Italian's systematic and determinate arguments on the classical principles of proportion and decoration naturally appealed to Jefferson's disciplined and orderly mind. Here was something that, like a well-founded legal system, one could count on. Jefferson found in Palladio a sustaining authority for his own eclectic classicism. He believed the lofty values of reason and order could work their designs upon the visual environment, both architectural and spatial, to fashion compelling models.

Jefferson persuaded President Washington to select the designs for the Capitol and President's House through competitions. Advertisements for designs were drafted by Jefferson and inserted in newspapers in March 1792, with entries due by July 15. A few professionally trained architects responded, but most of the entrants were carpenter-builders with little or no formal academic training as designers. The eighteenth-century American traditions of the builder-architect who executed his own designs based on architectural pattern books and of the educated gentleman-architect whose designs for churches and public buildings were recognized by honorary rather than monetary recompense had not yet given way to the professional architects of the Old World and early nineteenth-century America.

Hampered by their provincial sense of scale and limited building methods, the American designers were incapable of responding, either conceptually or technically, to the monumental requirements imposed by L'Enfant's grandiose scheme. On July 18, 1792, after judging by the president and three commissioners (only one of whom had experience in architectural matters), first prize in the competition for the President's House was awarded with a $500 premium to the Irish-born and -trained architect James Hoban.

Hoban's source for the design of the White House was Leinster House (1745–51, Richard Castle, architect), originally the Dublin residence of the duke of Leinster and today the Irish parliament house. The design was a simplified, bookish version of a traditional, mid-eighteenth-century Anglo-Palladian palazzo, a horizontally oriented rectangle with a tetrastyle Ionic portico attached to the north facade and a colonnaded porch spanning the entire width of the south facade. The plan called for a large, square entry hall on the north on an axis with an oval room, resulting in a central, semicircular bow on the south. A large audience room traversed the entire east side, while three more-intimate public rooms were distributed along the south facade. Private family quarters were on the second floor.

Hoban was also engaged to supervise construction of his design. Building the White House presented no great difficulties, as it was a type familiar to architects and artisans alike—a mansion with no extraordinary structural features. The cornerstone was laid on October 12, 1792. During construction one floor was essentially eliminated, reducing the three-story residence to two stories raised slightly above ground in the contemporary French manner. Built of light brown Aquia sandstone from Virginia, the building was first whitewashed in 1797. Generally referred to as "The White House" by Jefferson's day, it was not officially so designated until 1902.

Although construction was incomplete, President and Mrs. John Adams took up residence in the President's House in 1800. "The house is made habitable, but there is not a single apartment finished," Abigail Adams wrote in 1800. "We have not the least fence, yard, or other convenience, without, and the great unfinished audience-room I make a drying room of, to hang up the clothes in."

Benjamin Henry Latrobe redecorated the interiors, landscaped the grounds in a picturesque manner, and added low, single-story wings on the east and west to provide for storage and other household necessities.

Throughout two centuries considerable effort has been expended to maintain the White House as a symbol of the republic, despite changing styles and tastes. This volume examines two hundred years of the arts, architecture, gardens, and changing ways of life in this venerable house.

With scholarly talents and imaginative approaches ten essayists, each a distinguished historian or curator, combine to dissipate the fog of fable and blurred distinctions between fiction and reality that have inextricably become part and parcel of the story of our most important national building.

William Seale has spent a large part of his professional career researching and publishing magisterial works on the White House, in addition to a seminal volume on state capitols. We begin this book with his reconsideration of change and continuity in the physical structure of the Executive Mansion, plans that were realized and proposals that went awry. He argues that not all occupants of the White House were pleased with the chaste classicism of the building, and discusses several proposed radical alterations to the structure.

Prior to the transportation revolution, heavy and cumbersome building stone had to be quarried reasonably near the building site. Lee H. Nelson recounts how blocks of stone for the building of the President's House were cut, dressed, and hauled from the Aquia Creek stone quarry down the Potomac River in Stafford County, Virginia. Further, native artisans and craftsmen lacked stone-working skills; Nelson explains the ways and means by which stonecutters and masons were solicited and imported from England and Scotland.

Drawing on literary sources, travelers' accounts, and official historical records, Barbara G. Carson explores the rituals of entertainment and social events in the early White House years. In the changing social order—as the new nation and public officials sought to invent traditions—ceremonial "levees" and "drawing rooms" were receptions, Carson shows, that took on great social and cultural significance.

In a museum city celebrated for its extensive holdings of visual arts, William Kloss asserts, the White House collection of paintings stands apart, as distinctive in character as in location. Assembled primarily by gift, bequest, and occasional purchase, this art collection reflects the history of the residence and the personalities of the first families that occupied it. The celebrated works within not only reflect American ideals and achievements, but also exemplify the two great subjects that have constantly preoccupied American artists: figures and landscapes.

The focus of Betty C. Monkman's essay is the evaluation of the changing interiors of the White House. Looking back over nearly two centuries and buttressing her thesis with massive documentation, Monkman shows that the White House was never a series of static, museum-like period rooms, but constantly in a state of flux according to the whims, tastes, and eccentricities of the first families. Ever since John and Abigail Adams first occupied the house in 1800, successive administrators have been more likely to impose innovations and transformations on the interior, from republican refinement to Victorian splendor, than to dictate cohesiveness and continuity.

Replacement of interior furnishings in the nineteenth century resulted as much from changing decorating styles and tastes as from wear and tear. William G. Allman traces the history of presidential patronage, from John Adams to Theodore Roosevelt, of decorating services and durable goods from local vendors and craftsmen, as well as from well-known firms in the established centers of fashion—Baltimore, Philadelphia, and New York. Though Washington could satisfy most decorating needs of the White House with locally made furniture and silver, the city could not fulfill all the whims and fancies of successive first families.

At the beginning of the nineteenth century it was not unusual for the president and his family to find themselves surrounded by the appendages of a working farm in an untidy landscape of kitchen garden, apple orchard, stables, servants' quarters, and storerooms. Suzanne Turner recounts the evolution of this "garden of democracy" into the more formal grounds we know today, established during the administration of Millard Fillmore. The landscape of the White House has been laid out and planted, designed and redesigned over time, using ornamental horticultural elements and following instructions taken from popular garden literature and husbandry manuals.

The architect Charles Follen McKim transformed the White House physically and symbolically in 1902 during Theodore Roosevelt's new imperial presidency. Richard Guy Wilson contends that these renovations and redecorations during the so-called American Renaissance converted the Executive Mansion from a residence into a setting for ritualistic pomp and pageantry. In returning the house to its classical roots, McKim's work reveals both his own polemical nature and the intense nationalistic spirit of the nation.

The home of American presidents is a unique combination of private and public place—a family residence, a seat of government, a ceremonial center, and a historic building and museum. Marjorie A. Hunt has recorded the oral histories, personal experiences, and recollections of household staff who have worked behind the scenes to run the White House smoothly and efficiently. Her evidence indicates how the unique occupational setting of the White House shaped these individuals' work experiences, through which themes of family, home, and tradition run strong. A large body of accumulated knowledge resides in these reminiscences of work techniques and routines, of traditions of service and decorum, and of codes of behavior passed down from older to younger workers—the key source of continuity over decades of change in the White House.

The chief White House usher, Gary Walters, closes the book with a firsthand account of how the Executive Residence is cared for today. Nearly a hundred staff members carry out the desires of the president and his wife as they relate to the functions of the residence as family home, historical site, and location of official and ceremonial functions. Caring for 132 rooms and receiving hundreds of thousands of visitors each year, Walters must coordinate the operations of the White House with numerous other governmental agencies and orchestrate the work of his immediate staff of seven, the mechanical and maintenance staff of thirty-four, a domestic staff of thirty-eight, and the specialized group of professional curators, calligraphers, and florists.

From these varied essays we see that the White House is not a mere relic; unlike a fossil or an archaeological artifact, it is valuable actually because it was not petrified and so has not survived in its original, unaltered shape. The living and ever-changing White House has come down to us not because it is a historical building, but because it is a living building.

WENDELL GARRETT

— ONE —

The White House:
Plans Realized and Unrealized

WILLIAM SEALE

I T WOULD be difficult to imagine a house more continually fascinating than the White House. Most historic houses have their moments in the sun, then live on in relative obscurity. No house has been the scene of more important moments than has the White House. Its inhabitants are the most famous people in the country at the time they live there. Everyone is interested in what they think, what they say, what they eat, what they like, and what they do not like. Life in the White House fascinates us for the backstage view it provides of history.

The president has unquestioned control over the house and its contents. Congress may draw the purse strings, but over a span of two centuries Congress has refused few presidential requests regarding the White House. It is as truly the "President's House"—the earliest name—as it is the White House, the nickname it gained early in the nineteenth century and carried until the autumn of 1902, when Theodore Roosevelt made it official and put it on the stationery.[1]

All presidents recognize the power and mystique of the White House's past and, soon after they move in, find that they must adjust to the house as much as it to them. It is their home and their stage as well. The house will stand in the background of history's memory of them. Various minor alterations, often as simple as interior decoration, are made to the house in the course of adjustments to living there. Major changes, on the other hand, are usually the result of necessity, not the personal wishes of the individual in office. A chief of state may be in residence only a short while, yet effect permanent changes at the White House. Certainly this was true of Jefferson. Lincoln, by his presence and the melodrama of his life there, sanctified the White House; his changes were not architectural. Theodore Roosevelt demanded change, but turned the problem over to others. FDR found great pleasure in a constant program of changes, planned in part by himself, pencil in hand.

The presidents who made radical changes have been few. Their efforts give a form to the history of the White House, a history very different from the orthodox sort of architectural history. It is more akin to personal history, involving as it does the prerogative of the man in office. Only one president ever set out do the White House harm: Chester Arthur, who wanted to raze it altogether. Typically, change has come for the sole purpose of making the house work better for what it was built to do—though, of course, to varying degrees of success.[2]

Thomas Jefferson would have liked to build the house for the president. This, and all the details of the new capital, could have been considered the secretary of state's job. He had in mind a small capital city with a forumlike arrangement of public buildings, the same general scheme he had proposed for the state of Virginia at Richmond. The Virginia plan had fallen short of his entire concept, and only one of the buildings was being built.[3] Repeated efforts to revive the idea in the building of Washington were thwarted, as the project turned to the grander, more traditional visions of President

George Washington, who took the matter of the federal city into his own hands.[4]

Washington, ardently wanting the city to be built on the Potomac River, realized that it might require his personal prestige to make it happen. Time and again he stepped into the process, just to keep the ball rolling. He wanted no forum of Rome, or anything less than a great city built on the pattern of the European capitals. It would symbolize the great nation established in the Constitution. Just as he knew America would grow to fit its expansive form of government, so would the government, in Washington's view, grow to fit the city he had in mind. The city's location was central to the United States, and Washington believed that the Potomac River, with improvements, would become the avenue of commerce for the riches of the Ohio country to the sea.

The president's control of the project was tight. He appointed three of his most trusted friends commissioners of the federal city. For his architect he selected Pierre-Charles L'Enfant. "I have received him," Washington wrote, "not only as a scientific man, but one who added considerable taste to his professional knowledge. . . . He [is] better qualified than any one who [has] come within my knowledge in this country, or indeed, in any other, the possibility of obtaining whom could be counted upon."[5]

L'Enfant had come from France to fight for liberty, among Beaumarchais's volunteers, and had stayed on to seek his fortune among famous friends. He had dazzled the doubtful citizens of New York with splendid fêtes that helped promote the new Constitution and carry it to ratification. It was L'Enfant who had transformed the gloomy old City Hall into the beautiful, neoclassical Federal Hall, the seminal building of the Federalist age. On its portico General Washington had taken the oath of office as president of the United States.[6]

The Frenchman was on the scene at the Potomac already in the spring of 1791, mere months after passage of the Residence Act. Besides designing the city, he was to design public buildings. Among those last, as specified in the act, was a house for the Congress and a house for the president. By the time Washington joined L'Enfant there, the designer was bewitched by the possibilities in his assignments. He wrote that he found in the terrain, with its ridges and distant river views, "many of the most desirable position offer for to Erect the Publique Edifices . . . from these height every grand building would rear with a majestied aspect over the Country all around and might be advantageously seen for Twenty miles off."[7]

His city was built, essentially the Washington we know today. But his public buildings are largely forgotten. It is not known to what extent he had committed the buildings to paper, but the Capitol and the president's "pallace" were approved by the president probably in the fall of 1791. From them Washington seems to have gained his strong preference for stone construction. The President's House, which concerns us here, was sited on the location of the present house—a little to the southwest of where L'Enfant intended, but he yielded to Washington's preference, bringing the structure over the edge of a steep ridge—and digging for its cellars was well under way by the end of the year. New York and Pennsylvania avenues were laid out to frame the palace. The building was to be of dressed stone, its ground measurements approximately 700 feet east to west and 350 feet north to south, about four times the size of the present White House.[8]

L'Enfant's plan made enemies for him, not least of whom was Thomas Jefferson, who attempted to coax the commissioners toward his forum idea, as well as his preference for brick construction. But it was probably less his enemies than his own imperious acts that cost L'Enfant his great work. Constant clashes with the commissioners and landowners in the area led to his dismissal early in 1792. His palace was not built, but it lingers dimly in the historical record as the first and grandest White House plan that was never realized.[9]

The president, extremely worried, suggested that L'Enfant be rehired, lest the city fall behind schedule. Jefferson persuaded Washington to hold a competition for designs for the buildings and wrote the advertisement, although failing to specify stone construction. Washington, lukewarm on the competition idea anyway, began making his own inquiries about builders. This resulted in a Philadelphia conference with James Hoban, a young architect and builder whom he had met in South Carolina the previous year. Hoban, from Ireland, had impressed some of Washington's Charleston friends with his talent. Trained under Thomas Ivory, the well-known Irish architect, at the Royal Dublin Society's school in Dublin, Hoban had a thorough knowledge of Anglo-Palladian design, as well as construction in stone. His Charleston patrons had made it a point to bring the builder to the attention of the president, who had architecture very much on his mind.[10]

It is clear that some agreement on a design for a house was made between Washington and Hoban in Philadelphia in the spring of 1792. Without returning to Charleston, Hoban went to the federal city site and drew his competition entry in the offices of the commissioners. That July, the president selected Hoban's as the winning entry from a large number of other entries, most of which remain unknown today. Hoban's design was based quite directly on the palace of the duke of Leinster on Kildare Street in Dublin—a gentleman's seat, which Washington believed appropriate for the first gentleman of the United States.[11]

At the site some time later, Washington personally sited the building by driving the stakes in the ground.[12] The new plan being only a quarter the size of the place allotted to it, Washington decided to push the building wholly to the north and center it in the east-west line. This is the location of the White House. Hoban's plan was modified from the original Leinster House in several ways. As Jefferson had in his capitol at Richmond, Hoban exchanged the Corinthian order for the Ionic, as being easier for the American stonemasons to carve. On the interior the plan, while reflecting that at Leinster House, was greatly simplified, deprived of antechambers and most service halls. An oval "saloon" or principal room was built on the south, projecting as a bow from the south facade. Externally, the stone walls of

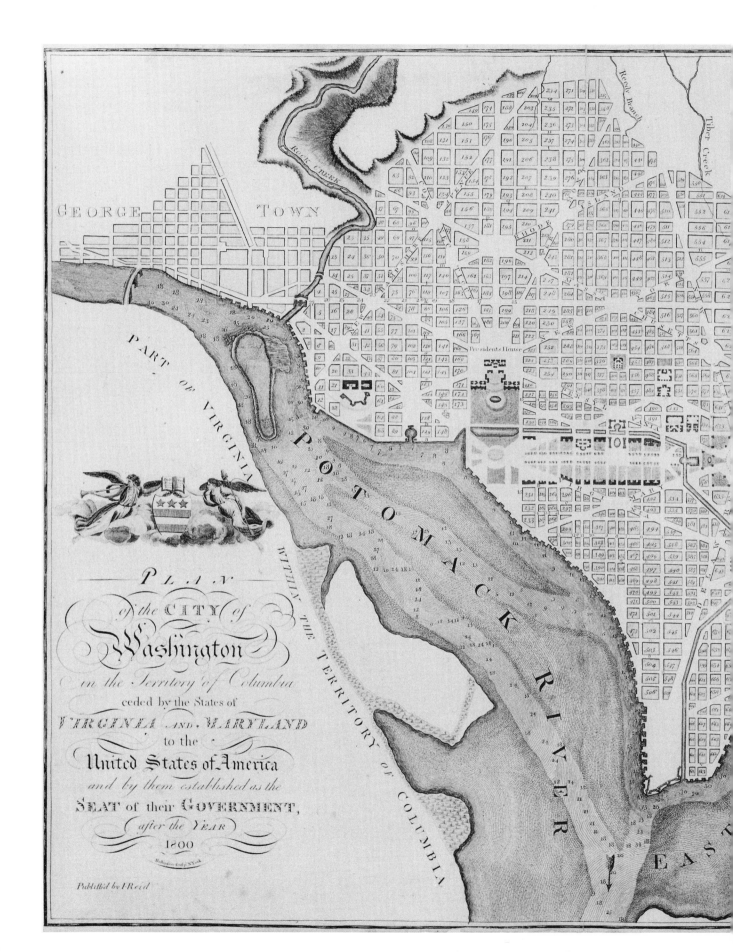

GEORGE TOWN

PART OF VIRGINIA

WITHIN THE TERRITORY OF COLUMBIA

ROCK CREEK

POTOMACK RIVER

Reedy Branch

Tiber Creek

RHODE

Presidents House

EAS...

PLAN of the CITY of Washington in the Territory of Columbia ceded by the States of VIRGINIA AND MARYLAND to the United States of America and by them established as the SEAT of their GOVERNMENT, after the YEAR 1800

Published by I. Reid

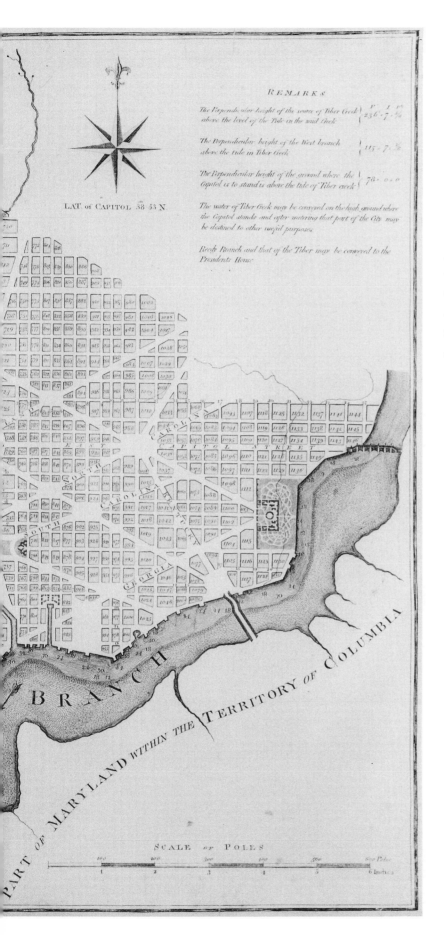

Plan of the City of Washington, D.C., by Thackara and Vallance, printed in 1792 (1800 imprint). When Congress selected the Potomac River for the ten-square-mile federal district, the Residence Act of 1790 stipulated that Congress would move to the new seat of government in 1800. It gave President George Washington the authority to oversee the erection of the public buildings therein, which was to be directed by three appointed commissioners. The city was named in his honor in September 1791, and he devoted an enormous amount of his time during the last decade of his life to the federal city.

the house were to be more richly carved and ornamented than those at Leinster House, and at last, toward the close of 1793, the "rustic" or raised basement level was removed from the north front.[13]

Thus adapted, the White House was built. Washington watched its construction with great continued enthusiasm. Several weeks before leaving office in 1797 he drove the stakes locating the public office buildings to the sides of the White House, to assure that they not be built adjacent to the Capitol, where the Congress wanted them.[14] This time he had consented to brick construction with stone trimmings, in the interest of cost, and to respect the current fear that the Aquia stone quarry downriver in Stafford County, Virginia, would play out.

The White House was occupied on schedule, on November 1, 1800. The last Federalist president, John Adams, lived there only about four months. He soon yielded to Thomas Jefferson's revolution in the election of 1800, which would set the pace for the nineteenth century in a presidency reduced in power and proportions. Jefferson, the first full-term occupant of the White House, lived there for two terms. No house could have been more opposite to what he thought appropriate. Yet he made every effort to put it to good use. Among his first orders was to assemble a suite of George Washington's tatty red-covered furniture in the Oval Drawing Room, that he, like the house, might identify with the hero.[15]

Jefferson may even have developed an affection for the house. At first he huddled in a corner of the main floor, but by the time he departed in 1809 he had filled the house, except for the East Room, which was not finished architecturally. He designed wings to the sides, which opened off the main floor like terraces, barely seen on the north, but on the lower grade to the south presenting neat colonnades. Plans were made for doing more, but were dropped in preference to work at the Capitol, which he believed it essential to complete. The house was already white with a coat of white-wash.

Under Jefferson's successor, James Madison, the White House was

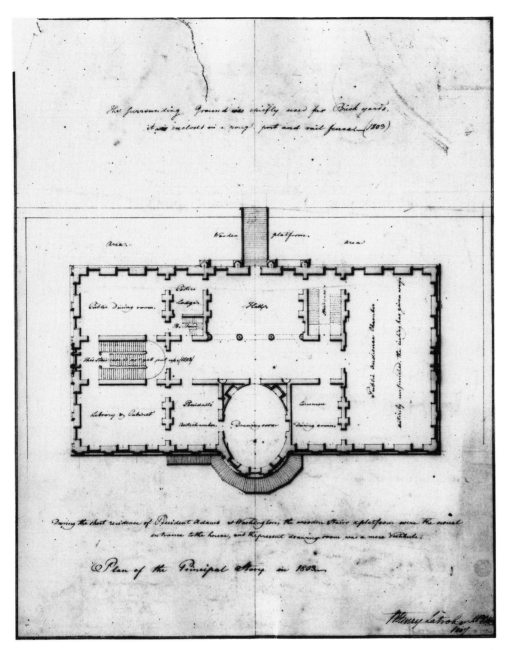

Benjamin Henry Latrobe's 1803 drawing of the principal floor of the White House, with the rooms designated as Jefferson used them. The erratic, English-born Latrobe was devoted to his patron Jefferson, but he did not have a high opinion of the president's architectural ability and was frustrated that he stuck so close to his "old French books" on architecture, "out of which he fishes everything." Latrobe's relationship with the White House would continue on and off from 1803 until 1817.

PLANS REALIZED AND UNREALIZED

The presidents house in the City of Washington, Sept. 1811

The President's House, probably by the English-born architect Benjamin Henry Latrobe, 1811, during James Madison's administration, showing Jefferson's east and west wings and the platform over the areaways. This was the north or public front of the White House. This scene is probably idealized in part: it is not certain that the eagle ornaments were ever acquired, and while the high stone wall was built on the south side of the house, none was ever put up on the north.

WILLIAM SEALE

burned along with the unfinished Capitol during the British invasion of 1814. When the war was over, the question arose of moving the capital to Cincinnati, a more central location. Proponents of staying put used the public buildings as a main reason for staying, such an investment having been made. When it was decided to remain, therefore, it became imperative to reconstruct the buildings as they had been, particularly the White House, which had been complete. Madison, and later, although less passionately, James Monroe, cast aside all rival ideas and pursued the reconstruction to its last stroke of white lead paint in the final days of the year 1817. Included in the reconstruction plans were columned appendages to the north and south. First built under President Monroe was the south "portico"—without a pediment and therefore technically a porch—in 1824 and on the north the portico ordered by the Senate Committee on Public Buildings in 1829 in anticipation of the coming to office of Andrew Jackson.

The White House remained largely unchanged thereafter for eighty years. There were to be alterations, of course. Comforts appeared almost as they were invented. Running water was added in 1833; central heating in 1837; gaslight in 1848; an elevator in 1882; electricity in 1891. Conveniences were brought in from the earliest time, from service bells to dumb-waiters to a telephone in 1879 and a typewriter in 1880. Pipes and wires were threaded through walls. Heavy bathtubs strained the wooden floor joists. Coat after coat of paint, layer after layer of wallpaper and carpeting found application through each presidential generation. Some old furniture went out to auction while new furniture took its place. Presidents and their wives brought their pictures to hang on the walls, where they grew crowded, frame-to-frame, a chorus of the past to greet each new occupant. The old gaslights were wired for electricity, then, obsolete to modern taste, were replaced with fine electroliers in the French styles of Washington's time. Still, James Monroe's silver remained in place, used nearly every day, and clocks of his purchase ticked away on the marble mantels of the parlors.

The first threat to the White House came in 1867 when the Army Corps of Engineers, fresh and numerous from wartime and eager with public improvements projects, proposed a new White House in the area we know as Rock Creek Park.[16] Lincoln's tenure during the dark years of the war had left the house in shambles. A new house was actually designed, although the drawings are lost. It was to be a suburban mansion with deep porches, set in the large and picturesque acreage, with miles of pleasure drives and walks. Many estates in the region were considered, but this location seemed the best. President Andrew Johnson approved. He left office, however, in 1869, and his successor, General Ulysses S. Grant, dismissed the plan en-

James Madison, painted by John Vanderlyn, 1816. In Madison, Vanderlyn found a sitter whose personal reserve matched the artist's style. The portrait's strength is in its simplicity. Rarely has a man's character been more clearly expressed in his face; Madison's penetrating, dispassionate intellect is as much in evidence in his head as in his aristocratic aloofness. His face is set above a high-collared black coat between a freely painted cravat and the simple powdered hairstyle favored by Madison. As one of the authors of *The Federalist*—"the best commentary on the principles of government, which ever was written," according to Jefferson—he went on to become "the father of the Constitution." When President John F. Kennedy was presented at the White House with the multivolume biography of Madison written by Irving Brant, he remarked that Madison is "the most underrated of our presidents."

tirely, preferring to make his residence at the traditional White House, Abraham Lincoln's house.

It was a house much used. The office had occupied rooms in the eastern end of the second floor since at least 1818. With the Civil War all the rooms of the east end of the floor, including the east hall, to which one stepped up over the East Room, contained offices. The telegraph came into the house in 1865, and by 1889 the office staff of twenty-five to thirty crowded uncomfortably beneath dangling electric bulbs, desk touching desk in corridor and room alike. Only the president had his own private office in this suite. Another room was devoted to the cabinet, although it had temporary occupants when the cabinet was not there. For peace and quiet the president often retreated to the adjacent oval room, which was the family library.

The family quarters consisted of seven rooms and two baths, and, after 1869, a sitting room in the west end of the central hallway. Normally the family used a small service stair that connected all the floors and the basement of the house. The grand stair was open and landed in the west sitting hall. It was not so much that there was no privacy as that one had the *sense* of there being no privacy. On the main floor, which was first open to visitors in 1801, the press of tourists had stretched viewing hours by the 1880s to six days a week. At public receptions, some six thousand persons were admitted, and the East Room's carpeted wooden floors were shored up from the basement with timbers. Stairs were put up to a north window, so guests could escape the suffocating interior.[17]

Chester A. Arthur, who became president on the death of James A. Garfield in 1881, found the house wholly objectionable and went to a friend's house while taking steps to demolish the White House. Torn up from temporary uses during the two agonizing months Garfield lay dying, and torn up from an interrupted interior-decorating project, the White House did look bad. Arthur had no luck at all, and the result of his effort proved that Congress would play no part in any plan to demolish the White House then or later. Arthur planned a large addition, which Congress would

PLANS REALIZED AND UNREALIZED

This photograph reveals a crowded but luxurious second-floor office in the White House ca. 1890, during the administration of President Benjamin Harrison. The female stenographer in the rear center is Alice Sanger.

not fund. At last he resorted to an interior redecoration, finishing out the contracts Garfield had made and calling in Louis C. Tiffany to do the rest.[18]

Practical needs were sometimes more readily resolved. Perhaps the most monumental appeared in 1889, when the Benjamin Harrisons moved in with their children and grandchildren. They were packed into the family quarters most uncomfortably, and the resolute First Lady, diminutive Caroline Harrison, no stranger to politics, took her plight to Capitol Hill. Senator Leland Stanford of California, chairman of the Senate Committee on Public Buildings, lent an ear. His power in the Congress seemed to justify her in thinking big. After a few weeks of consulting with officers of the Army Corps of Engineers, Mrs. Harrison produced a plan for a White House expansion program. Leaving the old house as it was, she envisioned wings to the east and west, and yet more wings headed southward, connected by a long greenhouse on down the slope. Hers was an ingenious plan: vast new space, and one could still stand in the Blue Room and see the river. Wise political thinking was seen in the roomy offices, public drawing rooms, and "national art gallery," all part of the grand plan. The family quarters would have some thirty rooms, with convenient baths.[19]

Stanford introduced the bill with the idea that it was in celebration of the one hundredth anniversary of the inauguration of George Washington and that it was a realization of the hero's original dream. Unquestionably the Harrison plan would have been funded had it not been for a political slip on the part of Senator Stanford. He did not approve the appointment of a postmaster in rural Maine. Speaker of the House Thomas B. Reed of Maine paid him back by killing the White House appropriations bill. Mrs. Harrison's decline from tuberculosis and death in 1892 might have ended the program, but it was kept alive by the Army Corps of Engineers. Through the next two administrations the engineers improved their plans. Grover Cleveland gave a half-hearted nod. William McKinley said he would think about it, as the nation prepared for the Spanish-American War in 1898.

The year 1900 marked the one hundredth anniversary of the first occupation of the White House. This time the corps, under Colonel Theodore A. Bingham, had left no stone unturned. The resolute colonel had written to the Royal Dublin Society, which had acquired Leinster House from the Fitzgerald family in 1815, and inquired about additions and alterations they had made. He was supplied with plans for two very large rotunda-like wings that had been added to the sides and forward, creating a forecourt to the old palace of the dukes of Leinster.[20]

Working with Frederick D. Owen, an engineer on his staff who had made the drawings for Mrs. Harrison, Bingham produced a grand plan for a visible, external expansion of space, which involved building monumental wings to the White House that, somewhat like the wings at Leinster House, terminated in great columned "Pantheons." On the east the wing was an office building tailored to McKinley's astute management of public information. Press rooms, an auditorium, a waiting room for bicycle messengers, and the inclusion of telegraph and telephone made this a top-notch communications center, as the art was known in 1900. On the west was the "state" wing, with new hotel-style kitchens beneath and state guest apartments above, with every comfort and convenience. Colonnades, parquet floors, stained-glass ceilings, and opera house magnificence, the Bingham plan was a true child of the new Library of Congress, Washington's most recent architectural wonder, for which the corps took full credit.

McKinley did not object. In November 1900 a lunch was held at the White House and a model of the grand scheme unveiled in the East Room. There was applause. A few present expressed utter outrage, notably Senator James McMillan of Michigan, who took a great interest in modern city planning. By neglecting to consult with him on this project, the Army Corps of Engineers had made an enemy in this embarrassed politician, who, in the Congress, was considered the last word on matters in building and architecture. Representatives of the American Institute of Architects, already threatened by this advent of engineers onto what they considered their turf, soon called on McMillan to protest. The senator calmed them with assurances that funding would not be forthcoming.

Then, in September 1901, President McKinley was assassinated in Buffalo, New York, and his vice president, Theodore Roosevelt, became president of the United States. McKinley's personal direction of the war with Spain in 1898 had wholly transformed the presidency from the relatively weak Jeffersonian mold into the powerful head of state not known since George Washington. The idolized leader was replaced by a young man of forty-two, a bombastic public figure, but one lacking in the public's eye the substance always assigned to the late president. It was thus up to Roosevelt to build up his own credibility while dramatizing the powerful and international character of the new presidency.

Privately, the Roosevelts, with a large family, were uncomfortable at the White House. They warmed to the plans of the corps, but other influences soon played on them, not the least being the author Edith Wharton, who was a self-styled expert on interiors in the Beaux Arts mode, and the American Institute of Architects (AIA), maneuvering through Senator McMillan. In the winter of 1902 the Bingham plan was overthrown and the design for remodeling the White House put in the hands of Charles Follen McKim of the Manhattan architectural firm McKim, Mead & White, designers of the Boston Public Library and so many other prominent buildings as to make them the leading Beaux Arts architects of the day.

An entirely different approach now was made. This grand plan was not only to revise the house, give it more room, and update it in every way, but also to restore it as well. McKim was entirely in charge. While his partner William R. Mead made the contracts, neither he nor Stanford White participated, insofar as is known, in the design. Normally McKim tested his ideas with Glenn Brown, director of the AIA and a gifted colonial revivalist who had both restored and built buildings of the historical sort. The two pared the White House in their minds to its basics. In this sense they "restored." Beyond that, they made it work, but not through large additions. The resurrection of Jefferson's east wing, with a small addition to it, and the building of a discreet office structure on the west were the only new parts of the revised White House. All other expansion was in the existing envelope.

The White House and its functions were rethought. Facts of White House life were brought into consideration: large crowds, the need for adequate family quarters, the desire for more conveniences, and the need for more office space.

McKim wished to keep the main floor more or less historical in character. To the need for coatrooms and rest rooms he responded by enlisting the grimy basement floor and transforming it into a ground floor. One modern kitchen with pantries replaced two early ones built for banquets and everyday use. Dingy servants' quarters, meat room, furnace room, and storage rooms were brightened and reborn as rest rooms and sitting rooms adjacent to the central corridor, which was groin vaulted, now plastered and painted white. The handsome result kept the auxiliary spaces off the main floor above.

The reconstructed east wing became the new social entrance, with the north door now a residential entrance. Callers passed through a loggia into the colonnaded wing, which overlooked an intimate garden; to the right was a large coatroom, and on ahead the colonnade joined the central corridor of the ground floor, whence a stair led to the main or state floor. On the west a temporary office was built at the end of the west wing, which still stood, and offices were removed from the second floor of the house. Originally, the temporary office was for the president's secretary and staff, not the president, who maintained only a work space there. Not until World War I would official ceremonies, bill signings, and the like take place in this building, for the presidents all preferred the historic ambiance of the house for historic events and important interviews.

Upstairs the entire second floor became family quarters. Bathrooms were added in the corners of rooms. The long transverse corridor, divided into three parts by arches, became a living area, off which the bedrooms and the oval library opened. New space was created by the combination of the grand stair with the business stair, near the East Room, so that no stairs now rose into the central corridor.

On the state floor the plan was the same, except for the removal of the grand stair. Where the old grand stair had been, the State Dining Room was

Aerial view of the White House, ca. 1927, during the administration of Calvin Coolidge. The Army Corps of Engineers had found structural trouble in the roof; this photograph was taken just before the old roof of Hoban's timber structure of 1817 was torn away and the old attic enlarged into a third floor with guest rooms, utility rooms, and a special "sun parlor" for Mrs. Coolidge. The work was done under the architectural advice of William Adams Delano of New York.

extended into a large room, second in size only to the East Room on the opposite side of the house. The decor was changed from the neoclassical of early America to, in the dining room, rich carved-oak paneling in the Georgian mode and, in the East Room, painted wood paneling designed after a room in the Louis XVI apartments of the Château of Compiègne in

France. Old carpeted floors were torn out and replaced by oak parquet, lightly bleached and waxed. Joliet stone paved the entrance hall, with its soaring white walls, its Doric cornice, and its monumental Doric columns.

The three parlors, the Red, Blue, and Green Rooms, more nearly reflected the historic house, their white woodwork with its richly carved corner blocks and the polished mahogany doors carefully restored, their walls, once papered, now stretched over with silk and velvet. McKim had little use for the antiques of the White House, and only through the intervention of Edith Roosevelt, an inveterate antique collector, were any of the old furnishings saved, unless they were French. In the Green Room, caned Adamesque furniture painted cream color was upholstered in floral chintz, while in the center was one of the round tables Andrew Jackson put in the East Room in 1829. The Blue Room was austere, from its mantel, copied from one at the Petit Trianon, to its cobalt silk walls and circle of white-painted furniture. In the Red Room the president and Mrs. Roosevelt intervened and had tufted red velvet sofas and chairs in the Victorian manner, the furnishings climaxed by a vitrine containing part of Mrs. Roosevelt's doll collection.

The renovation of 1902 was a remodeling indeed, but more significantly, it was an intelligent, logical rethinking. A house almost impossible to use was made functional in every sense: as a home, as a public house, and as a symbol of the presidency. The general external aspect of the house was the same as that built by Washington in the 1790s; the state floor was not radically different and, if more "international" in character, still felt about the same. McKim's was a master Beaux Arts approach to treating a historic building. The reverence for the past in such work is selective. McKim hoped to capture the essence of the White House in a new version of the same idea. His sensitive touch can still be felt in the White House today, even through the work of the heavier hands of engineers who would come along and remodel fifty years later.[21]

Major improvement came again in 1927, when the entire attic was removed and rebuilt larger in steel and concrete, beneath a steeper roof than before. When President Calvin Coolidge's new "third floor" was thus completed, there were two public floors to the White House, the state and ground floors, and two private floors, the second and third floors. Tucked away somewhat behind the parapet balustrade, the new third floor doubled the space available to the president and his family for servants' quarters, guest rooms, ironing rooms, or whatever use seemed necessary.

Meanwhile, the office building was doubled in size by President William Howard Taft, who built the first Oval Office in 1909. As plans were being finalized in 1929 for a second doubling, the office building burned on Christmas Eve; President Herbert Hoover ordered it reconstructed as it had been, as Madison had the burned house in 1814, to avoid the chance of public criticism in delicate political times. President Franklin D. Roosevelt took up Hoover's plans in 1934 and, with some variation, enlarged the West Wing, as it was being called, to twice the size, with a large part underground. He also built the Oval Office of today, near the Rose Garden.

Roosevelt delighted in architecture quite as much as Jefferson had, and he always had a building project under way at the White House. He had what amounted to a resident architect, Lorenzo Winslow, a National Park Service employee who by 1940 maintained an office and small staff in the White House.[22] Winslow met with the president frequently on little projects: a kitchen in the family quarters, a library on the ground floor, new picture arrangements, a new bathroom. With Winslow, Roosevelt began in 1939 an ambitious scheme for a large addition to the East Wing, in which he hoped to establish the first museum of White House history. The political climate seemed stormy, but immediately after Pearl Harbor, in early December 1941, the president ordered up his project, it was rapidly funded, and work began before Christmas. Although Roosevelt collected for the museum, the museum never came to be, and the space was quickly taken over for offices during World War II. By the postwar years, its usefulness in this way was well established and remained.

PLANS REALIZED AND UNREALIZED

Facing page: President Harry S Truman, photograph by Harris and Ewing studio, ca. 1945. Truman, a devoted student of American history, realized that the White House was more than timber and bricks, and took drastic steps to save the idea of the house that had sheltered all the presidents since Washington. The White House, Truman liked to say, was a place where "some lived it up and others wore it down." Between 1949 and 1952 the interior of the weakened house was dismantled and gutted to the stone walls, leaving only the 1927 third floor and roof structure, and a house of steel and concrete was built within the walls to support the roof. When President and Mrs. Truman moved back into the White House in March 1952, he had done what he set out to do: rebuild the house for all time. His renovation was the most radical in the history of the building. Madison and Monroe rebuilt it fairly exactly after it was burned during the War of 1812. Arthur had merely redecorated in the Aesthetic taste; Theodore Roosevelt's alterations were a revision of image and use in the Beaux Arts; Coolidge changed the roofline. Truman rebuilt the White House from inside out, and it remains today essentially as he left it.

———————————————

The last grand scheme for the White House had its seeds sown when the war began. Army engineers, ordered to the house, surveyed it with safety in mind. Their investigation was thorough. Crawl space between the ceilings of the state floor and the floors of the second floor was sufficient for access; not an inch of the house seems to have gone without study. The report declared the house a firetrap, laced with old, dry wood, crumbling mortar, and McKim's heavy, destructive steel. President Roosevelt, who liked old houses, dismissed the report as quickly as he dismissed the request by Civil Defense that the house be painted in camouflage. He did allow gas masks in the bedroom, and found much to mock in the sand buckets that came along as well. In defiance of it all, he lit the National Christmas Tree in his own backyard during the holiday season of 1941.[23]

The White House emerged safely from the war, only to find the engineering report looming over its future. When sudden cracks began to appear in the plaster and chandeliers began to sway by themselves, the report was produced and President Harry S Truman was urged to move out. Symbolic of all the trouble with the house was the sinking of the leg of Margaret

Truman's piano between two floorboards and into the plaster ceiling below. Truman moved to the Blair House across the street, and major decisions were made about the future of the White House.

The time was unfortunate for the old building in the antiquarian sense: the age of scientific preservation and conservation had not yet come. President Truman was interested in building, if not especially in architecture. He added the unhappy balcony to the south portico in 1947, asking no one's permission, and himself securing the sixteen thousand dollars it cost. Truman's balcony is a reminder that the president is lord of the manor at the White House and can do as he pleases with it. President Truman also had deep respect for the history the house represented. When faced in 1948 with the prospect of a significant structural renovation, he considered the distant future more than most of those who advised him: the real issue was whether the president would ever return to live in the White House. Truman, who attached so much importance to the symbolic White House, anticipated no other course than its perpetuation as official residence.

When this became clear to the planners, they had their direction. With the president's approval, they devised an ingenious scheme to save the stone walls but to empty them, literally as a pitcher might be poured dry, preserving doors, fireplace mantels, windows, fancy cast plaster, fine hardware, and other architectural elements for reuse. It was to be a virtuoso performance in engineering. A new White House would be built inside the old, without making so much as a damaging chip on the stone shell.

The makeover took place between 1948 and 1952. President Truman returned to a White House nearly doubled in useful space, equipped with the latest technology, and theoretically bomb- and fireproof with its thick shell of concrete and 660 tons of skeletal steel. Fifty-four rooms and some seventy service rooms gave the house the convenience of a first-class hotel, while it retained the familiar look of the White House. If McKim had partially replaced an American interior of wood and plaster with monumental materials, then Truman's renovation went the entire way. Very little was put back inside. The starkness of marble floors and walls gave the halls of the White House the chill of a public building, and even in the rooms where the floors were oak parquet, the steel construction contributed to a hardness not usual in houses.[24]

24

The White House today is essentially Truman's. It has undergone surprisingly few changes since 1952. There has been redecoration. While President Eisenhower permitted few changes in what he considered a new house, Mrs. Eisenhower had her way with the Diplomatic Reception Room on the ground floor, furnishing it in donated antiques of the early nineteenth century. Since then antiques have been brought there like offerings heaped on an altar. During the brief administration of President John F. Kennedy the state interiors were given a historical or period character that was highly theatrical, capturing the world's wholehearted approval. This was followed by Mrs. Richard M. Nixon's revision of the state rooms into museum rooms, which at this writing still survive as she had them, filled with a remarkable collection of American antiques, many with historical associations with the presidents themselves. To the collection of antiques has been added an excellent inventory of fine paintings. Historical objects, cared for in the most professional manner, have added a transient aspect to the timeless, symbolic White House. They are likely to move from room to room, from house to museum storage, as they are needed or not in use. The museum idea is the creation of our own time, and it marks, beginning in the second half of the twentieth century, a major change in the way the interiors of the house are decorated.

The White House will change again in major ways. The challenge tests the most creative imaginations. One always hopes changes there will be nearly invisible, and in their subtlety will follow the traditions of 1902 and 1952. Changes are made so that the White House will remain the President's House; its importance to the American people and to the president in his work merits the attention it gets. Needs of security—always a primary consideration at the White House—never remain the same, and today the house and complex appear too much guarded, like an armed fortress. Some adjustments will correct this, while preserving the necessary security. Some three thousand people form the president's staff, spread through three different buildings. Their practical needs increase and will be met.

PLANS REALIZED AND UNREALIZED

Workmen carefully raise a portrait of Woodrow Wilson above the Red Room's marble fireplace in 1952 as the rebuilding of the White House during the Truman administration moves toward completion.

WILLIAM SEALE

Change in methods and the use of innovations at the residence come more slowly than in the office wings, for the staff remains about the same from administration to administration and works well together, its patterns untroubled by constant turnover. Even so, new ideas do penetrate General Washington's thick stone walls. The computer has yet to become integral to White House life, but it has been in the White House since 1978, during President Carter's administration, and its work is increasing. Stringent modern standards of health and energy consumption have generally sharpened in the United States. Although matters for consideration for some years, they were not on the way to fulfillment at the White House until they became a personal interest of President Clinton.

In the daily operation of the house, questions arise and needs for change draw ever closer to definition. This is an ongoing process that through two centuries has been in a sense the same. As the President's House, the White House must function efficiently on every level, which includes the pragmatic as well as the symbolic (which itself becomes pragmatic here). At once a house of history and a modern machine for the presidency, the White House is unique. The mystique of the place comes from this compelling juxtaposition of past and present.

NOTES

1. George Cortelyou to John Hay, Washington, October 17, 1901, Roosevelt papers, Library of Congress.

2. The reader is directed to my book *The President's House: A History* (Washington: White House Historical Association/Harry N. Abrams, 1986) for an account of changes to and personalities at the White House from its inception to 1952.

3. Fiske Kimball, "Jefferson and the Public Buildings of Virginia, Part II, 1779–1780," *The Huntington Library Quarterly* 13 (May 1949): 303–10. See also Kimball's "Thomas Jefferson and the First Monument of the Classical Revival in America" (Ph.D. diss., University of Michigan, 1915; repr. in *Journal of the American Institute of Architects* 3, no. 9 [September 1915]: 371–81, 421–33, 473–91). Also, Henry-Russell Hitchcock and William Seale, *Temples of Democracy* (New York: Harcourt Brace Jovanovich, 1976).

PLANS REALIZED AND UNREALIZED

4. Records of the Commissioners of the District of Columbia, Minutes and Letters Received 1791–1792, passim. National Archives.

5. Washington to Commissioner David Stuart, Philadelphia, November 20, 1791, in John C. Fitzpatrick, ed., *The Writings of George Washington* (Washington: Government Printing Office, 1931–44), 31: 419–23.

6. The most known about L'Enfant can be found in H. Paul Caemmerer, *The Life of Pierre Charles L'Enfant* (Washington: National Republic, 1950). See also Elizabeth S. Kite, *L'Enfant and Washington* (Baltimore: Johns Hopkins University Press, 1929).

7. L'Enfant to Washington, Georgetown, June 22, 1791, *Columbia Historical Society Records* 2 (1899): 38.

8. The approximate dimensions of the "Pallace" are preserved in the locations of Pennsylvania and New York avenues, for the house was to be exactly sited at their extended crossing, so that the facades would be seen from the avenues. The "Dotted Line Map" in the collections of the Library of Congress further situates the house and its views as L'Enfant planned. Washington's locating the White House is found in his diary entries for June 28–29, 1791, in "Writings of Washington Relating to the United States Capital," *Columbia Historical Society Records* 17 (1914): 27–28.

9. All the details of the various clashes are chronicled day by day in the Commissioners' Minutes, National Archives, and the story is told by Caemmerer in *L'Enfant*.

10. Some biographical information on Hoban can be found in the minutes and records of the Royal Dublin Society in Dublin, but material on him is very scarce. His letters of recommendation survive in the Commissioners' Letters Received, National Archives. A case can be made that the courthouse in Charleston at the corner of Meeting and Broad streets, a rebuilding of a burned statehouse and itself called the statehouse for a century, was the building Hoban built that so impressed the Charleston friends of General Washington. I think it was this "statehouse" and not the one in Columbia, usually attributed to Hoban, that was actually his work.

11. Fellow students of Hoban in the Royal Dublin Society's drawing school published in 1780 a book showing Leinster House, and this Hoban may have shown to his client: Robert Pool and John Cash, *Views of the Most Remarkable Public Buildings, Monuments, and Other Edifices in the City of Dublin* (Dublin: Royal Dublin Society, 1780). See Washington to the Commissioners, Philadelphia, June 8, 1792, Commissioners' Letters Received, National Archives.

12. Commissioners to Mr. Johnson, Georgetown, August 3, 1792, Commissioners' Letters Sent, National Archives.

13. Commissioners' Proceedings, September 22–25 and October 22, 1793. See also Hoban to Commissioners, Washington, October 15, 1793, Commissioners' Letters Received, National Archives. The familiar "competition drawing," the earliest elevation of the White House, was obviously made a year after the competition, probably after the decision was made to drop the raised basement on the north.

14. Commissioners' Minutes, February 14–17, 1797, National Archives.

15. Margaret Bayard Smith, "The President's House Forty Years Ago," *Godey's Lady's Book* (November 1843): 212–13.

16. Benjamin B. French, *Annual Report,* 1864, the first time in print mention is made of the need for a new White House. General C. H. Michler, *Annual Report,* 1867, chronicles the search for a new site, and his letters sent and received in the Records of the Commissioner of Public Buildings, National Archives, provide the rest of the material, all complete except for the drawings for the proposed house.

17. This material is documented profusely in the records of the Commissioner of Public Buildings, National Archives, and in some instances, as with the receptions, in the local press of the time.

18. Tiffany's very detailed bill of October 2, 1882, is located in the Commissioners' Records (by this time the records of the officer in charge of the public buildings and grounds, but still generally called the commissioner), National Archives.

19. This episode, complete with letters and drawings, is found in *House Reports,* 51st Congress, #4042, "Extension of the Executive Mansion," March 2, 1891. See also Committee on Public Buildings and Grounds, *Report,* 1891.

20. Colonel Bingham's project is documented in his papers at the Library of Congress and in the commissioners' papers at the National Archives. See also Glenn Brown, *Memories* (Washington: W. H. Roberts, 1931).

21. The history of the McKim, Mead & White renovation is well documented, not only by their drawings and papers in the New-York Historical Society and drawings at the Avery Architecture Library, Columbia University, but in extensive photographs of high quality, which can be found in the collections of the National Park Service, Roosevelt National Historic Site, Sagamore Hill, Oyster Bay, New York. Copies are in the Office of the Curator at the White House.

Roosevelt's papers at the Harvard University Library contain correspondence by the family on the subject of renovations at the White House; the records of the commissioner at the National Archives are full and useful; Brown, *Memories*, tells the story from his, McKim's, and the American Institute of Architects' point of view. See also Senate Document 197, 57th Congress, *The Restoration of the White House.*

22. Papers of Lorenzo Winslow, White House Liaison Office, National Park Service, Washington. This large collection contains Winslow's unfinished memoir, which tells of his experiences with President Roosevelt.

23. Frank J. Wilson, Report, Washington, December 14, 1941; memorandum from Mr. Gaston to Henry Morgenthau, Washington, December 15, 1941; Michael F. Reilly to Frank Wilson, Washington, December 16, 1941, Franklin D. Roosevelt Library.

24. The principal source for the Truman renovation is the papers of the Commission for the Renovation of the Executive Mansion, 1948–1952, National Archives. On completion of the work, the commission published *Acts and Estimates: Reconstruction of the White House and Report* (Washington: Government Printing Office, 1952) for distribution to libraries and the public.

— TWO —

Crafted from Stone

LEE H. NELSON

AMERICANS tend to think of the White House as a symbol of the presidency rather than an example of early American craftsmanship. Yet, when seen close up, the building surprises and impresses most visitors, who are surprised at seeing such delicate ornamentation carved out of stone and impressed because such craftsmanship adds a new dimension to our appreciation of the White House as a landmark building. While a number of stories can be told about building the "President's Mansion" in the 1790s, this story is limited to what it took to "carve" this stone building two hundred years ago.

The construction of the President's Palace, or the President's House, as it came to be called, was placed in the hands of three commissioners appointed by President George Washington. Their job was to plan the work, secure cost estimates, find the necessary materials and workmen, pay the bills, and be responsible for the timeliness and the costs of the project. These three unpaid commissioners—Judge Thomas Johnson, David Stuart, and Daniel Carroll, all distinguished men—were accountable to President Washington, who took a strong personal interest in the project. Though the government was seated in Philadelphia during the ten years (1790–1800) when the federal city was being built from scratch, the president was kept well informed of the progress, and he made his own demands upon the commissioners. Even though he knew that the next president, not himself, would be the first to occupy the "palace," Washington carried out his own vision for the building, one that would be appropriate to the new nation. He wanted it to be large and built of stone, rather than mere wood or brick. The construction of a large stone building along the Potomac, where there was no established stone industry, would create almost insurmountable problems, plaguing the commissioners for years.

The commissioners had much more than the stonework to manage, for there were many other tasks associated with building the federal city. But overseeing just the stonework for the two most important buildings, the White House and the U.S. Capitol, would become a formidable task, as neither suppliers nor craftsmen were available to the commissioners in the new federal city. Knowing only that the building was to be large and made of stone, they took steps to get the work under way even though no actual plans existed and an architect had not yet been selected.

THE STONE PROBLEM

In the late eighteenth century, large cities such as Boston, Philadelphia, and New York had established stone industries, using local or regional stone quarries, with the necessary infrastructure to freight the rough or cut stone by land or water transportation. Philadelphia boasted a variety of local stone types to choose from, including marble in a range of colors. Such stones were used in a variety of ways, including fine architectural stonework cut for decorative features such as door and window trim, staircases, classical columns, and fireplace mantels. No such craft or industry, however, existed in or near the newly created District of Columbia. Much of the stone that had been used for architectural trim on eighteenth-century buildings in

Virginia and Maryland had been imported already carved from England, such as Purbeck or Portland stone. It would have been relatively easy to build of brick, as there was a plentiful supply of good clay. But the president wanted stone.

Outcroppings of stone along the Potomac River had been long known and used. One of these outcroppings was along Aquia Creek, some forty miles south of the newly created District of Columbia. This stone had been used for many years, but never on a large scale. The Aquia stone was selected by the commissioners for both the White House and the Capitol building, primarily because the quarries were served by water transportation, making the stone relatively accessible to the building sites in Washington. Even though it was unclear whether the quarry could meet their expectations, they leased the property and began to extract stone for the foundation walls of the White House prior to the preparation of architectural designs or drawings.

THE AQUIA CREEK STONE QUARRIES

The Aquia Creek sandstone used for the White House was commonly known as a "freestone," meaning a stone that can be worked freely in any direction because the grain or bedding layers are not sufficiently pronounced to interfere with the splitting, cutting, or carving of the stone. It is principally composed of quartz sand, with pebbles and pellets of clay, all cemented together with silica. In color, the Aquia stone ranges from a tawny white to a soft pink with streaks of rust caused by mineral deposits. The soft cementation makes the stone easy to cut and to carve. Unfortunately, this softness also contributes to poor weathering. Since it had been used for tombstones and architectural trim on various buildings in tidewater Virginia for nearly a century before the White House was built, the issue of weatherability probably received little attention.

Aquia stone was being quarried from several locations in Stafford County, Virginia. Small quarries situated on a fifteen-acre island astride

Aquia Creek would eventually supply most of the stone for the White House. Although the creek is quite wide at this point, it is also quite shallow. Only at high tide could ships load the rough-cut stone blocks and transport them down the creek to the Potomac River. From there they could sail upriver to the new city.

The island had been acquired in the 1670s by George Brent, and it remained in the Brent family for generations. Another George Brent, a descendant, deeded the land to the commissioners in February 1792. Presumably, the Brents had opened the several small quarries sufficiently that both the quantity and quality of the stone was evident to the commissioners. To develop the quarrying operation for the capital, the commissioners needed a much larger operation, requiring additional labor, equipment, and transportation.

A SCOTSMAN TAKES OVER

In April 1792 a Scottish master mason named Collen Williamson was contracted to serve as overseer. His duties were twofold. In Stafford County he was to develop and expand the modest operation at the quarry in order to provide a large and reliable stone supply for shipment to the federal city. In Washington he was to supervise the laying of the quarried stone for the foundations of the building, once the exact site and design of the building were established. Without an architect or a final design for the White House, it was all rather chaotic at this stage.

Collen Williamson seems to have been the right man for the job, at least initially. Sixty-five years of age, he was an experienced master mason from the village of Dyke, in northeastern Scotland. Coming from a family of stonemasons, he was accustomed to operating as a "master builder" in the traditional meaning of the term. Why he came to the United States at that point in his life is not known, but it was probably owing to the same economic difficulties that led other skilled craftsmen to migrate to America during the next several years.

It was likely that Williamson took over a sporadic quarry operation with

LEE H. NELSON

A stone carver at work with his chisel, tooling furrows into a piece of stone, a craft technique used on the ground floor stone walls of the White House. Seen here are the typical tools of the trade, including the carver's workbench, square, level, mallet, pick, straightedge, dividers, chisels, trowel, and frame saw (on the ground at the lower left). Also visible are typical specimens of the stone carver's art, including column capitals, bases, moldings, and mortuary work.

relatively low production. Initially, the order from Pierre-Charles L'Enfant (then in charge of laying out the city and its principal buildings) called for ninety-nine thousand cubic feet, or more than eleven million pounds of stone, just to build the foundation walls. That was roughly twice the amount finally needed, but L'Enfant had envisioned a much bigger building than was subsequently built. To begin this enormous task, the commissioners hired "twenty five able bodied negroe men Slaves to be employed at the quarries." Williamson had to teach the slaves the task of quarrying. The names of these quarry workmen have gone unrecorded. We know only that they were allowed a diet of pork and bread, with a daily ration of one pint of whiskey for each man. Working the stone would be a long and dangerous task, continuing through the long, hot summer days and the cold winter months.

CRAFTED FROM STONE

QUARRYING THE STONE

Williamson's task was to continue the quarrying operation on the island in Aquia Creek, but on a much larger scale. Vegetation had to be cleared away to expose new stone surfaces. Usually, the upper reaches of the exposed stone were of little use because the stone was damaged by vegetation, tree roots, and the continual splitting and heaving caused by frost over time. Using considerable labor, the damaged stone surfaces were cleared away and discarded. When it appeared that they had reached good stone, the quarriers used labor-intensive techniques to free relatively large blocks of stone. First, they chiseled (actually picked) a vertical face on an outcropping of the stone, which would serve as a working plane from which they could measure and begin to plan the removal of blocks of stone. Using hand picks, they then cut two trenches four to six feet deep into the stone, perpendicular to the face of the stone and roughly ten to twenty feet apart. Then a rear trench, connecting the two side trenches, was cut behind and parallel to the initial stone face, effectively creating a very large rectangular mass of stone that could be split into manageable sizes. To minimize waste, these trenches were only about twenty inches wide, providing barely enough room for a man to work with a pick and cut a relatively smooth surface on each side of the trench. Nevertheless, there was a lot of waste in the overall process, from the clearing away of flawed stone to the debris created during the trenching process and the rough cutting of blocks to size.

Weight and handling were factors of major importance. Each cubic foot of stone weighed about 120 pounds. As a result, each stone that was quarried for use in the walls above the foundation was ordered in dimensions corresponding to a specific use, such as for the wall, cornice, balustrade, or other locations. These dimensions were only slightly larger than actually required, reducing weight for shipping and handling while allowing for final trimming at the job site.

After the blocks were cut at the quarry, each was marked with identifying letters and numbers, and then probably hoisted onto wood sleds and dragged by teams of oxen down the hill to the stone loading dock at the northeast corner of the island. There they would be loaded by crane onto small ships for shipment down the Aquia Creek and up the Potomac River, some forty miles to the federal city. Three sailing ships, the *Columbia,* the *Ark,* and the *Sincerity,* were used to transport the stone. Each was capable of carrying more than thirty tons of stone.

Millions of pounds of stone blocks thus were laboriously split out of the quarry for the White House, cut to useful sizes, dragged to the water's edge, loaded onto a barge or boat, sailed to Washington, unloaded, and hauled to the stonecutter's workshop at the building site, only to be handled several more times before they were finally placed into the walls.

LAYING THE CORNERSTONE

Before any stone carving could get under way at the White House, two problems had to be resolved. First, there had to be a design for the Presidential Palace with drawings that would show the appearance, the details, and the dimensions. Second, highly skilled stonemasons needed to be brought to the federal city. The first problem was more easily resolved than the second.

Thomas Jefferson, then secretary of state, had a lifelong interest in architecture and strongly believed that the best way to get a distinguished design was to hold a competition, a practice that was little used in this country but that was common in Europe. Jefferson drafted newspaper announcements for two competitions, one for the Capitol and one for the President's House, and obtained approval from President Washington. Dated March 14, 1792, and published in the country's major newspapers, the announced competition called for entries to be submitted before July 15 and offered a prize of five hundred dollars or a medal of that value for the winning entry.

James Hoban won the design competition for the President's House.

Born and educated in Ireland, he was working at that time as a house carpenter in Charleston, South Carolina. For his award Hoban selected a gold medal and took the remainder of the prize in cash. Unfortunately, Hoban's original drawings and design have not survived; he subsequently modified the winning entry in order to meet the expectations and demands of Washington and the commissioners. Pleased with their choice, the commissioners subsequently awarded Hoban the job of directing the entire construction process.

On August 2, 1792, Washington came to the District of Columbia, surveyed the foundations, and drove the final stakes for construction. Excavations for the basement and part of the foundations for a much larger house had already begun under the orders of L'Enfant, who was locating the major buildings and laying out the city. It is not known how much of

An Ionic capital for one of the pilasters, typical of those on the south, east, and west walls of the White House. They exhibit delicately turned volutes, acanthus leaves, egg and dart moldings, and finely detailed cabbage roses, canted down toward the viewer on the ground.

LEE H. NELSON

these early foundations were built or what changes were needed to comply with the adjusted siting, but the work of laying the foundation stones, already delivered to the site from the quarry, was far enough along to arrange for an elaborate event to mark the laying of the cornerstone.

That event took place on Saturday, October 13, 1792, beginning with a parade. Starting in Georgetown, the commissioners and freemasons led all the various workmen, commonly called "artificers," to the foundations of the President's House, where they formally placed the cornerstone. Although its precise location has never been found, a newspaper account of the ceremony reported that the cornerstone was laid at the southwest corner of the building. An inscribed brass plate was embedded with wet mortar onto the top surface of the stone. The inscription was as follows:

> This first stone of the President's House was laid the 13th day of October 1792, and in the seventeenth year of the independence of the United States of America.
>
> George Washington, *President*
> Thomas Johnson,
> Doctor Stewart [*sic*],
> Daniel Carroll,
> *Commissioners*
> James Hoban, *Architect*
> Collen Williamson, *Master Mason*
> VIVAT REPUBLICA

After the ceremonies, the group marched back to Georgetown, where they celebrated with an "elegant dinner" replete with sixteen toasts, honoring every conceivable interest of the participants.

THE CARVERS FROM SCOTLAND

Even though enough of the foundation had been built to have a grand ceremony, the final design of the house was still unsettled. Expected costs were too high. Within two weeks, Washington approved a one-story height reduction, and the commissioners declared that the walls would be brick with a stone facing, instead of all stone. These actions dramatically reduced the cost and the amount of the required stone. But the commissioners faced yet another critical problem: few stone carvers were available to carry out Hoban's elaborate design for what was to be one of the first embellished stone buildings in the land. Though the commissioners had made earlier and futile attempts to lure stoneworkers away from good jobs in Philadelphia, New York, and Boston, they now had to expand their search and follow up on earlier efforts to obtain skilled labor from abroad.

In January 1793 the commissioners began a year-long search by sending letters to contacts in Great Britain, France, and Holland inquiring about tradesmen, including stonecutters. With war in Europe, this was not an opportune time to undertake the risky sea voyage to North America. Meanwhile, Collen Williamson proceeded with work at the White House, employing the few stonecutters he had and the additional laborers that could be trained. Despite the difficult work conditions and pressing schedule, Williamson's crew did a very creditable job, as evident from the finished stonework on the ground floor. All the stones except for the bold projecting window enframements were neatly dressed, with hand-tooled vertical furrows covering their entire surface.

By eighteenth-century standards, the White House was to be a very large building, measuring 87 feet wide, 170 feet long, and 53 feet in height, with foundations five feet deep and walls constructed of quarry-faced blocks of Aquia stone. Though intended to be an all-stone building, only the exterior walls of the ground story were constructed all in stone, over four feet thick. Because of cost constraints, the upper two stories were to be a combination of brick and stone: a brick back-up wall and a thick stone facing. Yet even these upper masonry walls were quite an achievement, measuring three feet in thickness.

Given the quality of the stonework on the ground floor of the President's

House, it is unfortunate that we know so little about Collen Williamson's crew at that stage. About all we know is that Williamson claimed to have started the work on April 8, 1793, and had completed it by August 7 of the following year—an impressive accomplishment.

The ground floor was entirely faced with thick blocks of cut and tooled stone, backed by rough-cut stone. In addition, the ground floor windows had molded architraves and bold rustication around the windows. This amounted to 514 lineal feet of stone walling, twelve feet in height and four feet thick, which required that almost three million pounds of stones be quarried, transported, and worked by hand. Despite this impressive start, the most difficult and skilled part was yet to come, requiring a team of talented stone carvers.

In their efforts to obtain the services of skilled craftsmen, the commissioners authorized a Philadelphia merchant named George Walker, who was traveling abroad on business, to search for stonecutters in England and Scotland. In London, Walker published a broadside to attract craftsmen to the new federal city. According to the broadside, the commissioners were offering the prevailing rate for work and would pay the sea passage for stonecutters to come to America, even providing an advance to cover expenses while at sea. Single men were preferred, but the same travel arrangements applied to wives.

Walker's efforts met with no success in London, and he went on to Edinburgh some months later. This was a good time to recruit stonemasons in Scotland; by 1793 a number of building projects had come to a halt owing to the economic effect of Great Britain's entry into the European war. In Edinburgh, Walker was successful in attracting an experienced builder and stonemason named John Williamson, who was perhaps related to Collen Williamson. In addition, six other members of the same masonic lodge—Lodge No. 8—George Thompson, James White, Alexander Wilson, Alexander Scott, James McIntosh, and Robert Brown—agreed to come to America and work on the White House. From 1794 until 1798, when their

CRAFTED FROM STONE

stonework ended, there were some ten to twelve stonecutters working at the President's House. Other known stonecutters from the federal pay records were Alexander Reid, James Reid, Andrew Shields, and Hugh Sommerville.

Even with the enlarged work force, the stonecutters needed considerable assistance. Unlike other craftsmen at the White House such as the carpenters, the Scotsmen objected to using slaves as hired help. Reluctantly obliged in this respect, the Scottish stonemasons were allowed to follow tradition and take on white apprentices. The Scots were more flexible than English craftsmen, who were more stratified in their craft and specialties. In Scotland, stonecutters were also masons, capable of laying stone, a skill of particular value in the labor-short work force in America. With the additional skilled labor and apprentices now available to Collen Williamson, work settled into a busy routine consisting of ten-hour days, six days a week.

When the quarried stone, ordered according to size and location for the White House, arrived in Washington, it was then hauled over land to the large stone yard and sheds on the presidential grounds, north and east of the present building. When they arrived, the stones were inspected for proper size and quality. The architect, James Hoban, estimated that one eighth of the stone from the quarry was not usable and had to be reordered.

While Hoban designed the building, Williamson worked out the details and figured how to actually build the structure. A complex maze of stonework was involved as well as a tremendous logistical effort. There were few identical pieces of stone, and thus little opportunity to mass-produce similar pieces. Except for the ashlar, which were the plain rectangular blocks of stone between the windows, most stones were unique. On the south wall alone, approximately forty distinctly different kinds of stone needed to be cut: window sills; window architraves with moldings and "ears"; decorative consoles under the window sills of two different types; window pediments of two different types; carved support brackets under the pediments; pro-

Ionic capitals on the columns of the north portico, an addition constructed in 1829–30. The stylized rose petals of this later addition lack the naturalism of the petals on the original pilaster capitals on the south, east, and west walls of the White House.

CRAFTED FROM STONE

jecting pilasters that varied in width from top to bottom; elaborate pilaster capitals carved in the Ionic order with scrolls, cabbage roses, and leaves; a full classical entablature consisting of a molded architrave, hundreds of stone dentils and modillions, a crown molding, round balusters for the roof railing, and the cap stones. And these are just a few of the examples and some of the variations. Nor does this take into account the right hand/left hand variants; the special conditions that occur only at the corners; or the special carvings on the other facades, including ribbons and bows, oak leaves, and garlands.

Every piece was preordained for its place in the building. This was something that the master mason had to plan and manage independent of the architect, even though the architect was in charge of the entire operation and the two had to work together closely. Williamson made what are today called shop drawings, which spelled out details such as moldings and construction joinery, enabling the craftsmen to carry out the architect's concept. Using the architect's designs, Williamson and his successor, George Blagden, submitted written estimates to the quarry, ordering the blocks of stone to be delivered to the stone carvers at the President's House. Their listings identified the necessary pieces of stone by name in priority order, the number of each piece, and its length, breadth, and height.

TOOLS, LOGISTICS, AND SKILL

The incredible variety of cutting and carving was done with about a dozen different tools, including an assortment of hammers, axes, picks, chisels, and stone saws. In addition, there were levels, squares, straightedges, and a great variety of special templates, plus the usual tools for mixing mortar.

The stone arrived from Aquia with "quarry-cut" surfaces, a rough dressing of closely spaced pick marks evening out the surface irregularities from the quarrying and splitting of the stone. Without further work at the job site, this quarry-cut surface was too rough to serve as the exposed face of any stones at the White House, although it was suitable for use on the

The lunette window over the front or north doorway. The enframement of rich stone carving includes consoles, engaged columns, and arches ornamented with a mixture of oak leaves, acanthus leaves, medallions, and griffins. Above the entrance are high relief carvings of ribbons, bows, and swags of oak leaves and acorns accented with roses.

hidden or back surfaces and as foundation stones. The work of finishing the surfaces was delegated to the helpers and apprentices, along with other tasks such as sawing the ashlar wall stones and squaring them to size. Special work such as carving the moldings, balusters, and Ionic capitals was done by the stone carvers.

Each stone followed a forming sequence depending upon its use and placement in the building. Flat surfaces were usually created by sawing the stone, a tedious task indeed. The saw consisted of a large U-shaped wooden frame fitted with a thin, toothless blade that was stretched between the two

A general view of the large lunette window and Palladian entry centered on the west wall. The central portions of the east and the west walls were damaged beyond repair during the burning of the White House by the British in 1814; they were rebuilt in 1816 under the direction of the original architect, James Hoban. The stone details in these sections are believed to match the original construction. The lunette window is framed in stone with a kneed or bracketed molding, a large scrolled keystone with a projecting acanthus leaf, and large acanthus leaf brackets supporting the windowsill.

ends of the wooden frame, not unlike a modern coping saw. The blade was drawn across the stone while wet sand was placed between the blade and the stone; the cutting was thus an act of abrasion. In areas of the stone where a saw could not be used, flat surfaces were made with a hammer and a drove, a square-edged chisel about two or three inches wide. To make flat surfaces with such a tool required a good eye, a straightedge or template, and a controlled use of the hammer.

Once the stone was carved, the finish was applied. Some finishes added texture to the stone. For example, tooth tooling, used on the basement stones, produced parallel and closely spaced furrows. Most of the stones on the upper walls had smooth surfaces, which were produced in several stages. After the face of the stone was hand dressed or made flat with a chisel and checked with a straightedge, it was then honed smooth by rubbing the surface with a smaller flat stone and abrasive sand.

In addition to the variety of skills involved, heavy manual labor was required in handling the stones during the cutting and carving process, and during the construction of the wall. At the White House, two large wooden derricks, about fifty feet high, were moved around the building as needed. These wooden derrick poles were similar to those used at the quarry and were equipped with pulleys and rigging to help lift and place stones on the building walls. To lift the stones into place, a dovetailed rectangular slot, approximately three to six inches deep, had to be cut into the center of most stones. Commonly known today as a "Lewis hole," the cut was made in the top face of the stone. It permitted iron wedges on a hoisting ring to be fitted into the slot and held in place with a center spacer. After the stone was lifted up and installed in the wall, the iron wedges were removed. Then the hole either was covered by the following course or, in areas where it was exposed to weather, such as a window sill, was partially filled with wood or hemp and sealed with mortar.

Installing the stones required considerable skill. Stones ranged in weight from about three hundred to over three thousand pounds, yet despite the difficulty of moving such stones into place, many of the stone joints are only about one-sixteenth of an inch apart or less. There was little room for error in the cutting or fitting. Applied while seating the stones, the lime and sand mortar provided little more than a thin "bed" to keep the weather out of the joint.

THEY LEFT THEIR MARK

Pride, craft, and self-identity have long been inextricably intertwined. Stonecutters were no exception. Mason's marks—geometric designs composed of triangles, Xs, arrows, and crossed straight lines—were carved into the stone to identify the work of the individual craftsman. Generically called "banker's marks" because similar symbols were widely used by merchants to identify goods and products, their use can be traced back to the Middle Ages. Whether on churches, palaces, or fortifications, mason's marks are commonly found on early stone buildings in Europe. In America, they appear primarily on buildings and engineering works dating from before the 1840s, when their use declined.

In eighteenth-century Scotland and England, "operative" or working stonemasons granted a mark to apprentices upon completion of their training as a symbol of the knowledge and worth of the new mason. In many cases, the granted mark was a variation of the teacher's or master mason's design, providing a history and background for the future employer. Registered and protected by the mason's guilds or lodges, the marks served a practical purpose when the extent and complexity of the work were "measured" to determine the costs to the owner, based upon certain rules governing the specific charges for different kinds of stonework.

More than thirty characters have been found and recorded during periods of renovation and alteration at the White House. These marks are the signature of stonemasons who worked on the White House during the 1790s, as well as the partial rebuilding after the 1814 fire, and during the addition of the north and south porticoes in the 1820s.

LEE H. NELSON

The windows of the first floor of the White House have alternating triangular and arched pediments supported by large consoles. The second floor windows have kneed or bracketed architraves or moldings and acanthus leaf brackets supporting the sills.

Most of the White House mason's marks are neatly carved on the back or hidden surfaces of the building stones, unseen until the stones were removed during alterations or restoration work. During the extensive renovation of the Executive Mansion in the 1950s, many mason's marks were discovered and the stones removed. Some were distributed by President Truman to state and other masonic lodges in North America, while a number of the stones were retained and the marks displayed in two reconstructed fireplaces on the ground story of the White House.

CRAFTED FROM STONE

Looking at a White House mason's mark is perhaps the closest we can come to identifying with the person who carved any part of the handsomely skilled stonework. It is his signature.

FLOWERS, LEAVES, AND RIBBONS OF STONE

The process of carving the stone into delicate shapes such as flowers or leaves is practically indescribable. While there are few written descriptions of such skills being performed in early America, the finished works of art remain. Their beauty and vigor are marveled at and appreciated even after the effects of two hundred years of weathering.

The carver needed to plan carefully and to visualize the finished product. There could be no mistakes. Before taking a tool in hand, the craftsman had to plan the approach to carving the pieces down to the most precise detail. As the unwanted stone was chiseled away, the delicate rose petals or other features were gradually revealed. This was sculpting, a form of fine art in every respect. The delicate carvings executed at the White House were a tribute to the achievements and talent of the stone carvers. Largely unnoticed for the past two centuries, they are deserving of the recognition and appreciation given to exceptionally high levels of craftsmanship.

The more elaborate pieces of stone carving consist of designs well known to students of classical architecture, in the eighteenth century as well as today. These more elaborate details, some of which are illustrated here, include the following:

LEE H. NELSON

Guilloche: a chain of interlaced curves around a series of circular voids. Bands of guilloche appear under each window on the first floor of the north, east, and west walls.

Fish-scale imbrication: a pattern representing the overlapping of fish scales. This decoration is used on supporting brackets under the window sills of all the first-floor windows, except for those on the north facade.

Acanthus leaf brackets: a carved bracket depicting an acanthus leaf. They were used under the first-floor windowsills on the north wall, and a slightly different style of acanthus leaf bracket was used under the sills of all the second-floor windows. Another elongated version is seen supporting the pediments of the first-floor windows.

Griffins: mythical creatures resembling winged lions. Two are centered in the inner arch of acanthus leaves over the north entrance doorway.

Ionic capitals: column or pilaster capitals decorated with scrolls, cabbage roses, eggs and darts, and acanthus leaves. They are used atop all pilasters and columns. In the center of the capital, the rose petals are the most high-relief carvings on the entire building. Tilted downward to give the causal observer a three-dimensional view, the boldness and complexity of these carvings are barely apparent from the ground.

Ornament was not limited to classical architectural features. Common items became subjects for permanent decoration on the White House and made the mansion more American. These applications include the following:

Oak leaves and acorns: features from the great American forests were intertwined in the outer archway band over the north entrance doorway. They are also seen on the brackets framing the door.

Ribbons, bows, and swags: festive items of celebration. Two swags festooned with ribbons, two bows, two large roses, hanging bellflowers,

Detail of the north doorway, the front entry, richly enframed with the elaborate stone details of console (a long curved bracket supporting an entablature and pediment), acanthus leaf label corbel, or stop (a flowered quatrefoil), oak leaves and acorns from the great American forests, and a column capital decorated with acanthus leaves. Ornament was not limited to classical architectural features but included common items from America's forests, which made the mansion more American.

CRAFTED FROM STONE

oak leaves, and a central medallion are a major ornamental motif over the main north entrance doorway.

Additional carvings were made for the door and window architraves, and considerable time was required in constructing the building entablature and the extended roof cornice, which had more than three hundred large stone balusters under the capstones.

The heavy paint buildup over the years not only obscured the delicacy of these carvings but also created maintenance problems. Where the paint had failed owing to age and weathering, it admitted moisture into the wall and allowed deterioration of the stone. Starting in 1980, the systematic removal of these many layers of paint has allowed a fresh understanding and appreciation of these problems and indicated the steps necessary for their resolution and the restoration of the stonework. More than that, the newly exposed surfaces also provided a whole new appreciation of the many attributes of the original stonework, but especially of the carving and its three-dimensional qualities. The richness of the carving is evidence of the symbolic importance attached to the President's House. Along with the U.S. Capitol, it was unquestionably the finest stonework within the new nation, a credit to the president, the commissioners, the architect, and the stone carvers.

ACKNOWLEDGMENTS

This paper is based in part upon the research notes and writings of William Seale. The writer is indebted to Mr. Seale for sharing the notes in his files.

The writer also acknowledges the assistance of Timothy Buehner, Historical Architect, Technical Preservation Services, Preservation Assistance Division, National Park Service, Washington, D.C., for help at many stages of this project, including making sketches, drawings, and photographs, and especially for research efforts in connection with the Aquia quarry.

LEE H. NELSON

Rex Scouten, Office of the Curator, the White House, was very helpful in making the White House photo files available for study and publication. Those files are as interesting and useful as they are voluminous.

The writer also acknowledges the help, interest, and support of Charles Fisher, Historian, Technical Preservation Services, Preservation Assistance Division, National Park Service, Washington, D.C., for bringing this focus upon the White House stonework into reality.

FURTHER READING

This chapter has been adapted from a booklet by the author entitled *White House Stone Carving: Builders and Restorers,* U.S. Department of the Interior, National Park Service, Washington, D.C., 1992. This booklet contains additional information about the quarrying of the stone and about the restoration work being carried out by a small but dedicated crew of stonemasons.

McKee, Harley J., F.A.I.A. *Introduction to Early American Masonry, Stone, Brick, Mortar and Plaster.* Washington, D.C.: National Trust for Historic Preservation and Columbia University, 1973.

Seale, William. *The President's House: A History.* Washington, D.C.: White House Historical Association, 1986.

————. *The White House: The History of an American Idea.* Washington, D.C.: American Institute of Architects Press/White House Historical Association, 1992.

Withington, Charles F. *Building Stones of Our Nation's Capital.* Washington, D.C.: U.S. Geological Survey, U.S. Department of the Interior, 1981.

CRAFTED FROM STONE

— THREE —

Social Seasons and Rituals
of Entertainment

BARBARA G. CARSON

ALL CITIZENS of the United States, who possess the means [should] visit the capital of their country at least once in their life time," declares the author of a little book called *A Description of the Etiquette at Washington City,* first published in 1829.[1] People followed this advice and in the early national years took to the newly improved roads and turnpikes in carriages, stagecoaches, and even wagons. They journeyed on steamboats and later on trains to come to Washington. There, during the winter social season when Congress was in session, they stayed in boardinghouses, taverns, and hotels; saw the sights; and mingled with distinguished, fashionable, and wealthy citizens and foreigners. A cast of characters, real and imagined, tumbles off the pages of historical documents and fictional accounts of the city. They visited the White House on New Year's Day and the Fourth of July for "levees" or receptions, on scheduled evenings for public "drawing rooms," and by invitation at dinner parties.[2] Washington was the one and only American city where, on a few annual occasions, any properly dressed man or woman could enter its grandest and most famous house, walk through its elegantly furnished reception rooms, and sip lemonade or Madeira and eat cake and ice cream with distinguished personages. Fashionable hobnobbing made people feel good about themselves and optimistic about their country.

These official rituals in the early United States expressed the ambiguous practices and attitudes Americans held toward their new political structure and changing social order. While the procedure of extending invitations to dinners was straightforward, the process of self-selection of the company at levees and drawing rooms posed a mystery in the new democratic republic. These events, seemingly open to all, helped shape a national consensus about participation in politics at the same time that they articulated a separation of social groups and reinforced the position of those in power. Some in the capital city paid no attention, others observed from a distance, and a select few experienced the entertainments at the President's House.

Washington residents, congressmen and their wives, out-of-town guests, and foreign diplomats and travelers described events and personal experiences in the capital. Their words serve as criteria for judging the verisimilitude of the works of fiction discussed here: five novels, two of which are epistolary, and one of these in verse.[3] All are set in Washington, include White House vignettes, and were first published between 1820 and 1828, although two look back in time to the Jefferson and Madison administrations. Margaret Bayard Smith, a well-educated early bluestocking from New York, came to the fledgling city in 1800 as the bride of Samuel Harrison Smith, the publisher of Washington's first newspaper. The author of two of the novels, *A Winter in Washington* (1824) and *What Is Gentility?* (1828), she claimed her "descriptions of scenery and society [were] drawn with truth and fidelity, from the then existing circumstances of place and manners."[4] External accounts corroborate her assertion. George Watterston, a librarian of Congress, turned out two more. *The L . . . Family at Washington* (1822) and *Wanderer in Washington* (1827). Although more satirical than Margaret Smith's books, his novels are rooted in intimate experience with the details of the city's political and social life. The third author, who published his versified letters *The Fudge Family in Washington* (1820) under an "editor's" pseudonym of Harry Nimrod, has not been identified.

Unlike the presidents, congressmen, officials, local residents, and travelers who figure in historians' accounts of events in the early capital, the principal characters in these five novels are virtually unknown. They are worth scrutiny, however. For the most part they are rural folk of humble origin who are uncertain of their behavior in the new city. They believe, however, that they, and especially their children, can learn from experience, profit from exposure, and change for the better. They have enjoyed enough success at home to be confident of achieving more. Because the authors attribute motives to actions, the novels provide important additional insight into the human dramas played out in the early capital. Like their real counterparts, the fictional characters came to Washington to display themselves, marry their daughters to men of wealth and influence, seek offices, and promote positions that would offer them better economic and political opportunities. Their overblown hopes sometimes contrasted with their limited achievements.

The White House features prominently in each novel. Marriageable young ladies, established matrons, office seekers, influence peddlers, and government officials anticipated, participated, remembered, and reported about the rituals they attended—levees, drawing rooms, and dinners. Each of these functions had significance beyond its effect on these individuals' lives. The government of the United States had been established on new principles of political equality, however imperfectly they were realized. It had also eliminated the formal possibility of birth as a criterion of social ranking, although of course the well-born continued to benefit from prosperity and connections. For the sovereign people of the United States, every White House event carried the heavy weight of a national political and social symbol.

Elected representatives and bureaucrats brought to the new capital di-

President John Quincy Adams, painted by George Peter Alexander Healy in 1858. This was one of six presidential portraits by Healy commissioned by an 1857 act of Congress in an attempt to assemble a complete collection of presidents for the White House. Adams had sat for Healy in 1845; the portrait was painted after Adams's death.

verse ideas of who should rule politically and who should mix socially, and they did not always agree about matters of protocol or levels of luxury. They understood, however, that immediate political gain could follow from social encounters. In Smith's *What Is Gentility?* a senator and his wife debate the matter. She takes the aristocratic position and advocates a "court" circle where access is limited; he argues as a small-*d* democrat that the drawing room circle should be congruent with the sovereign power, that "the President was the people's servant, and the President's house, the people's house." The author (writing in 1828) comments, "In later years. these rights have been somewhat encroached on" because "aristocratical notions respecting rank in society are too prevalent in our country where no privileged orders exist." Therefore "it remains yet to be seen how far the people will be able to maintain their claims."[5] Smith did not anticipate the events of the Jackson administration.

Successive presidents sometimes fumbled as they experimented with George Washington's carefully considered model for entertaining in a democratic republic. Washington "adopted that line of conduct which combined public advantage with private convenience" and decided to receive visitors at his residences in New York and later in Philadelphia on three different weekly occasions. He invited guests, mostly members of Congress and their families, to dinners. On Tuesday afternoons between three and four o'clock he held formal receptions for men only. No food or drink was served. On Friday evenings at eight o'clock he and Mrs. Washington gave less-formal public parties. Special invitations were not necessary. The only criteria for admission were adequate clothing and the rudiments of polite behavior. The self-selected company was announced and paid respects to the president and his wife. Then, while the ladies were seated and the gentlemen walked about, servants passed trays with tea and light refreshments. There was conversation and music, but no card playing or dancing.[6] John and Abigail Adams followed these procedures and took them to Washington for the first congressional session held there, in the winter of 1801.

Changes that occurred in the first three decades of official entertaining to some extent resulted from the varied personal circumstances and preferences of the presidents. Their styles of entertaining also expressed the different political positions of these men. Federalists tended toward greater formality than Jeffersonian republicans or Jacksonian democrats. As the city grew and the number of people involved in the government expanded,

BARBARA G. CARSON

highly personal procedures simply took too much time, and some alterations in social practice were inevitable.

More than most presidents, Thomas Jefferson expressed idiosyncratic ideas about official entertaining. Perhaps because he disliked evening drawing rooms or perhaps because he was a widower and these occasions were clearly associated with the president's wife, he eliminated them and gave many more dinner parties. He seems to have considered dinners as relaxed occasions where rules of precedence were unnecessary. Notions of hierarchy that had formerly organized entry into the dining room and seating at table gave way to the confusion of each guest taking the place that was personally most agreeable. Some, especially Mrs. Merry, wife of the British minister, took offense with this "pell-mell" etiquette, and Jefferson had to explain his intentions and methods.[7]

Dolley Madison was long remembered for her personal warmth and hospitality. She paid calls on many ladies in Washington, making them feel welcome to come to the White House. They appreciated her reintroduction of "night levees" or "drawing rooms" as regularly scheduled public entertainments at which ladies and gentlemen milled about to the accompaniment of military music and the service of refreshments.[8] After the burning of the White House, she continued to give parties and squeezed her guests into the smaller spaces of rented presidential housing.[9]

President Monroe and his family moved into the refurbished White House in October 1817 but began the season's entertaining only with the New Year's Day levee. Neither Elizabeth Monroe nor Louisa Catherine Adams enjoyed Dolley Madison's popularity. The Monroes and the Adamses may have preferred to reduce their contacts with the general citizenry. Their actions also reflect a practical response to the expansion of government and the growth of Washington's population. After Mrs. Monroe ceased the practice of paying ceremonial visits, the ladies of Washington expressed their irritation. Secretary of State John Quincy Adams was forced to write a widely printed explanation justifying the decision.[10] During both

Dolley Madison, the wife of President Madison, is portrayed in this 1848 oil painting by William S. Elwell. As First Lady she was renowned for her personal warmth and hospitality. She introduced music and refreshments to White House gatherings known as "night levees."

of these administrations drawing rooms were held, but with less frequency. By 1829 at presidential receptions the two antechambers and three large reception rooms might be so full that E. Cooley in *A Description of the Etiquette at Washington City* advised guests to take food and drink "when an opportunity offers, which at some of the fullest levees, may not happen very often: not because there is any scarcity of refreshment, but [because of] the difficulty the waiters find in making their way through the crowd with their large trays."[11]

BARBARA G. CARSON

Although few described it, the White House was large and in many ways splendid.[12] Because the "company [was] in constant motion, especially during the session of Congress," the durability of carpets and other furnishings mattered as much as style.[13] Even so, the adjectives *fashionable* and *elegant*

Plateau and basket attributed to Denière et Matelin, gilded bronze and mirror glass, ca. 1817. President and Mrs. James Monroe refurnished the burned-out White House with imported French furnishings then at the height of fashion. The plateau centerpiece, with seven mirrored sections, measures 13 feet 6 inches in length when fully extended. Standing bacchantes holding crowns for candles or tiny bowls border the plateau.

were applied to specific pieces and the general effect. The two major furnishing efforts of the period—that of Dolley Madison and Benjamin Latrobe, which disappeared in the conflagration of 1814, and the more controversial Monroe replacement—emphasized the color crimson, which made some of the reception rooms "red as fire."[14] Elbridge Gerry, Jr., visited his father, who was vice president under Madison, in the summer of 1813 and described the oval drawing room as "immense and magnificent. . . . The windows are nearly the height of the room and have superb red silk velvet curtains. . . . The chairs are wood painted with worked bottoms and each has a red velvet large cushion."[15]

Citizens did not often protest the expenditure of federal funds for decorating the White House. The purchase of large quantities of French gilt furniture during the Monroe administration and John Quincy Adams's billiard table drew the most disapproval. When the public censured presidents for their selections of furnishings, they expressed two main objections. They did not like to see foreign goods in what was perceived as aristocratic taste in the president's house. In so far as possible, their head of state should live with American-made goods. They also felt that public money should not be diverted to equip presidents for personal pleasures. Generally, national pride encouraged a consensus about the importance of "marble pillars and pilasters" and "knives of silver and cut glass," even for a people's palace.

Paul Fudge, irritated by the French furniture and other extravagances, had more to say than most visitors, whether historical or fictional, about the effect of the decorating schemes.[16] He attended a dinner during the Monroe administration.

> But much I fear the nation's purse
> For what I saw will be the worse—
>
> . . .
>
> "A lantern with a red cravat,"
> Did you e'er see a thing like that?

BARBARA G. CARSON

With pictures, candelabras, vases,
Stuck about in fifty places.

. . .

State Rights in dishes prostrate lain.
Fly to the ceiling in Champagne;
Or in their grave, those rights laid low,
Beneath a thing they call plateau.

Because of short winter days and the hour that congress adjourned, most presidential entertainments took place after dark. The glow of light from candles and lamps reflected off silvered and mirrored surfaces; it shimmered and tracked the movements of real and imaginary guests as they paraded from room to room. Each member of the company, which represented a wide spectrum of the American population, felt entitled to join in the jumble. Foreign visitors with their rigidly hierarchical notions about social intercourse were completely confused, but also fascinated with the American experiment and its possibility of a different world order. Among Americans the "somebodies" may have held "aristocratic" notions and preferred more exclusive society. Occasionally, they expressed their wishes that the "nobodies" would dress better and behave less awkwardly, but they rarely scorned their fellow men and women as people or as potential political associates. Nor did they question their presence at a White House social event. Ordinary men knew it was their right to participate in the political process and to bid for government office. They and their wives caught the spirit of opportunity for upward mobility and dressed themselves as best they could for the hurly-burly of social life in the nation's new capital. A few were invited to dinner; many more showed up for the evening drawing rooms or the midday parade of the New Year.

DINNERS

"The President of the United States, requests the Pleasure of Mr. & Mrs. Baily's Company to Dine, on Thursday next, at 4 o'Clock, Jan. 1, 1801.

An answer is requested." So reads an invitation recording the first dinner party given by the Adamses at the White House.[17] In the years that followed many guests described dinners they were privileged to attend. Although these occasions were numerous in reality, in the Washington novels they occur less frequently than drawing rooms and levees; there are only two. Paul Fudge's rhymes offer details about the decor, table arrangements, menu, servants, service, and other guests, some of whom he ridicules for their social pretensions. Ichabod Coffin, an office seeker in Watterston's *Wanderer in Washington*, doesn't reach their level of awareness; lacking all dignity, he displays total ignorance of the world of official dinner parties.[18]

White House dinners were not casual events. Foreign ministers, heads of departments, members of Congress, special visitors, and personal friends were sent printed invitations in which blank spaces were filled in with the

President's House invitation, printed document and completed in manuscript, recording the first dinner given by President and Mrs. John Adams in the unfinished President's House on New Year's Day, 1801.

BARBARA G. CARSON

guests' names and the day, date, and hour of the occasion. Their wives were included regularly, which was probably somewhat unusual in the United States in these decades, because dinners tended to be masculine affairs.[19] Perhaps the expectation of the wives of foreign ministers that they would be entertained and the experience of many American government officials and their wives who had previously lived in European capitals explain the Washington custom. Perhaps it simply indicates a local way of expressing more general alterations in the lives of some women in the early nineteenth century.

Guests noted other kinds of changes at White House dinner parties. The old concept of a table first abundantly laid with many unadorned meats and a few plain vegetables cooked in traditional English style and then followed by a second course of puddings and pastry gradually was supplemented with a new interest in sauces and other complexities borrowed from French cooking. Not everyone approved of the new menu. Paul Fudge found

The table also little pleas'd me,
The names of dishes they so teaz'd me,

. . .

I did not see a dish I knew,—
Though those I know are not a few.

On the other hand, Juliana Seaton, wife of William Seaton, the publisher of Washington's *National Intelligencer,* enjoyed the "many French dishes, and exquisite wines" served to her at the Madison White House in 1812. She noted, too, the similarly innovative dessert course of "ice creams, maccaroons, preserves and various cakes," followed by "almonds, raisins, pecan-nuts, apples, pears, etc."[20] In a traditional meal many meats and vegetables were placed symmetrically down the center and around the edges of the table. Host, hostess, and guests with some assistance from servants helped each other to the food. French cookery brought *service à la français.* Substantial items on the menu were more likely to be set out on a sideboard than down the center of the table, which was filled not with food but with ornaments, sometimes an elaborate plateau with candlesticks, statues, and "castles of painted sugar work."[21] Since the new arrangement did not encourage self-service, more waiters or footmen were required.

Most of the domestic servants throughout Washington were African Americans, some slave, others free. Female servants worked behind the scenes, while male servants were in the public eye, riding postilion on carriages or assisting in dining rooms. In elite residences such as the White House, they wore livery. During his presidency Thomas Jefferson paid a tailor more than £18 for the materials and labor to make four livery coats.[22] He chose blue fabric with red lining and silver lace trimming. Red was another color favored for livery at the White House. Paul Fudge thought it incongruous that men who could wield strong axes were

> Set up with lace upon their backs:
> And those so fit for toting rails,
> Were patched with red down to their tails.

He emphasized their light-colored skin.

> You also see, arrang'd in queues,
> "White negroes" here, of ev'ry race,
> . . .
> And, worst of all, are dress'd in lace.

Although servants remain shadowy figures in the published novels, there are occasional hints that the authors think of them as knowledgeable observers and as critics of behavior.[23]

Paul Fudge emerges from the poem as a man of substance and gentility. He considers his invitation a personal compliment and tells some family history, a tale of upward rural mobility with which many of his fellow guests could probably have identified.

BARBARA G. CARSON

But thanks to one most lucky hit,

More than to our father's wit,

We present happy race of Fudges,

Whose plebeian ancestors were drudges,

   Bids fair to rise into renown:

Tis right, that each in turn, should sway,

. . .

For every dog should have his day.

Writing to his brother from the new city, he supposes that

. . . never did our mother dream,

   when feeding pigs or picking peas

Beside Piankitank's sweet stream,

   Her Paul would see such things as these;

Still less 't would ever be his fate,

To dine and drink with folks so great.[24]

The plodding verse hammers home the point that quite ordinary folk have emerged as participants in the nation's political affairs. They have exchanged backwoods behavior for conversation about luxurious international food and drink.

But Peter you'd have laugh'd with me,

If you'd been only there to see

Some folks disputing about wine

. . .

As if they had been us'd to dine

. . .

Though you and I remember well,

   That when last time we came across 'em,

They quarell'd, and to fighting fell,

   'Bout which was best, bear-meat or possum.

Paul Fudge focuses on the false refinement of his fellow dinner guests. In *Wanderer in Washington* George Watterston draws a broader distinction between dignified simplicity and low vulgarity.[25] He created the second dinner guest, one Ichabod Coffin, to be ridiculed. Inept, awkward, and very hungry, he does everything wrong. He arrives too early, bites into an artificial apple displayed on a mantelpiece, pours himself brandy, which he takes for wine, and instead of eating sweetmeats, thrusts the sugar radishes, plums, and candy "into his pocket, for a future occasion."[26] When he finally sits down at the crowded table, the food and service baffle him. He mistakes *blanc mange* for cheese and a leg of mutton for goose. The five soup bowls or plates brought to him during the first course disappear before he satisfies his immense hunger, and he asks the waiter, "Do you think a man can live on empty plates, or fill his stomach by looking at pretty dishes?" During the second course, the servants exploit his inexperience for their own amusement. They bring him a large piece of very hot pudding, which he greedily crams into his mouth. The inevitable pain brings forth a desperate call for water. Immoderate laughter from another guest distracts Ichabod's attention, and he involuntarily spews the hot pudding in that direction. The coarse and overdrawn mayhem promote the author's satire of the "tag rag and bob tail" company that might come together around a presidential dinner table.[27] It must be noted, however, that Ichabod had come as an invited dinner guest.

LEVEES OR DRAWING ROOMS

Martha Washington's "Levey Day" introduced in New York in August 1787 was a Friday evening party to which no special invitation was necessary. In Washington by about 1830 people also used the term *drawing room*. Announcements for these occasions at the White House were public, and admission was open to those with introductions, adequate clothing, and the rudiments of polite behavior.

On these evenings people talked with one another and sampled refreshments. "At the president's levees there is commonly no other amusement but conversation, so that . . . the presumed honour of being one of a party, of the highest order in the United States, are all the inducements that an entire stranger has to go there."[28] Mary Bagot, wife of the British ambassador, itemized the refreshments served at one of Mrs. Madison's evening parties as "Tea & coffee & afterwards cold punch with glasses of Madeira & cakes."[29] The menu may have expanded over the years, because in 1829 another writer added "jellies, ice-cream, and white and red wine, mixed and unmixed, and sometimes other cordials and liquors, and frequently . . . West India fruit" to the list of treats that liveried servants carried about the rooms on large trays.[30] Guests moved about as opportunity offered, women usually on the arm of an escort. The "loud and confused murmur of voices" overwhelmed them no matter where they roamed.[31] According to one critical visitor in 1810, some were "a little inclin'd to reel:—gigling, simpering & drinking, talking, hiccuping and bowing & scraping & walking, the sum & substance of the levee."[32] A major change occurred during the season of 1828–29. The "celebrated east room" was finished, although unfurnished. Music and dancing were added to the usual entertainments, and President and Mrs. Adams closed their last official evening party with a splendid supper.[33]

Levees or drawing rooms were important events because they told the sovereign people that their president was accessible. Wearing "small clothes" rather than court dress, formal attire, or a military uniform, he stood in the central oval parlor and greeted every man and woman who chose to spend the evening at the people's palace. The openness of evening drawing rooms raises questions about the social makeup of the guests. Since announcements were made to the public, did "all the world" show up? What necessary conditions and sense of self made an individual or a family feel entitled to attend? How did guests from various walks of life behave toward and regard each other?

In *A Description of the Etiquette at Washington City* E. Cooley wrote at some length about the company at these events. Although theoretically anyone could attend, "as very few people would attempt to go to such a place, without making a genteel appearance, and believing themselves, more or less, entitled to mix in such society, it is very rare that any but the most distinguished and genteel people are to be found there." On the other hand, he was quite comfortable suggesting that when seeking social opportunities, one could be decently aggressive. "At these levees any citizen of a fair character, and of suitable appearance for such a place, may, by proper management, ultimately succeed in being introduced to any individual that attends the levees and parties at Washington."[34] Cooley clearly implies that the criteria were imprecise and the barriers porous. Through the 1820s they created a process of self-selection that allowed Americans simultaneously to acknowledge equality and to practice selectivity.

Not surprisingly, in his etiquette book Cooley emphasized procedures such as making introductions, exchanging cards, and paying calls that set some guidelines for admission. Out-of-towners generally seem to have practiced what he preached. They scrounged introductions and latched on to someone who knew the ropes. In 1811 Washington Irving was distressed when most of his luggage, including his introduction to the Madisons, was on one side of the city and he, on the other, was dressing for the drawing room. At the last minute he found someone to scribble another letter, giving him the stamp of acceptability.[35] Even with these precautions, the makeup of the company could be unpredictable. George Watterston called one drawing room "a confounded hodge podge assembly" in which "secretaries and cobblers, members of congress, and shoe blacks [were] all mixed up together, like the ingredients in the cauldron of the weird sisters."[36]

Europeans, with their continuing belief in the rightness of a clearly hierarchical society, were fascinated and perplexed by this kind of social mixing. Occasionally they were offended. In a much-reported incident of 1806 Mrs. Merry, the wife of the British minister whom President Jefferson offended with his pell-mell etiquette at a White House dinner, was appalled to find she was to be introduced socially to her haberdasher at a party hosted by the secretary of state. Writing to his titled mother, Augustus Foster, then the young secretary to the British legation, asked her, "Were you so placed how would your Feelings have been shattered."[37]

What Is Gentility? offers an instructive example of the way Americans went about the process of self-selection.[38] Although one of the richest families in the city, the fictional Mr. McCarty and his wife did not go to drawing rooms. He had begun in business as a proprietor of a grog shop, literally living "over the store." The well-meaning and sympathetically drawn couple are decidedly not genteel. Both explicitly state that they had never been in a gentleman's house. Recognizing their own limitations, they send their daughter to a Philadelphia boarding school, where she develops social skills, airs, and a taste for society. She makes a friend whose father is an impoverished military officer. All gather in Washington, where the colonel, who counts on a good marriage for his daughter, schemes and arranges for a senator and his wife to boost the two young ladies socially. Under their guidance the girls exchange calls with Dolley Madison and attend one of her drawing rooms.

The scene in which Mrs. Madison comes to call at the McCarty house shows her understanding of people who have "bettered themselves" and provided advantages for their children that they themselves had never known. Dolley Madison's social attitude and behavior, described in yet another novel, were "altogether republican; and if she made any distinction at all, it was always in favor of such as were in the more humble walks of life, and might thus think themselves overlooked or neglected."[39] The visit greatly embarrasses the daughter, who, although she has learned drawing room manners, lacks true gentility and cannot comfortably enjoy her parents' vernacular ways.

A fine boarding school instilled in the fictional McCarty's daughter a sense of entitlement to attend drawing rooms and a longing to be admitted to the "first circle" of Washington society. Louisa Catherine Adams recorded

a real incident in which awareness of one example of upward mobility inspired its expectation. A coachman, who had just driven his employer, a "gentleman from New York . . . with his family and of great wealth," to a drawing room given by the Adamses when John Quincy Adams was either secretary of state or president, showed up as part of the company at the same party. Mrs. Adams does not say how he was dressed, only that he held a whip in his hand. When asked to explain his presence, he reasoned that since his master had once been a driver, "he thought therefore he had a right to be there also."[40]

While Europeans in Washington occasionally revealed their bewilderment or irritation with the uppity presumptions of a grocer's daughter or coachman, elite Americans were less ready to censure such attitudes or behavior. Although their social acceptance of bricklayers and cobblers and their sons and daughters may have been reluctant, many were coming to believe a more open society offered a better way to think and to act. Both Harriet Otis, the half sister of the wealthy Massachusetts politician Harrison Gray Otis, and Otis himself expressed their thoughts about the admission of more people to polite company and occasions. After she had been introduced to a printer "under . . . most remarkable circumstances," Harriet Otis wrote she felt her "pride a little hurt—but checked such rebellious risings as well as I could at the time and when such things are over they serve only for diversion."[41] Her brother, who had attended a private party, wrote to his wife that "It was a crowd and very much mixed—There are not a few persons who have misgivings, at this amalgamation of all ranks and degrees and who either absent themselves or go with reluctance—It amused me exceedingly to see who were there, and who were not."[42] Otis, like many others, had voted with his feet in favor of acceptance; he had gone to the party.

Fictional members of *The L . . . Family* prevailed on one of their congressmen to act as their "cicerone" or guide the evening they planned to attend a presidential drawing room. In reality, those in the know, especially congressmen, seem to have had no graceful way to refuse such social responsibilities. In 1812 a New York couple visiting the capital dredged up a memory of old acquaintance with one of their state senators, and although they had never met his wife, they appealed to her for assistance. She later wrote that politeness forbade her refusing to accompany them and that the pair "came away well pleased with the entertainment, and particularly so with Mrs. Madison."[43] In 1816 Margaret Smith initiated an inexperienced minister in the ways of drawing rooms. First, she insisted that he replace his boots with newly purchased shoes. After their arrival at the party, she showed him "how to take my hand and lead me in."[44]

The size and composition of the drawing room company was somewhat unpredictable. Fifty people was thin; three or four hundred, in the language of the century's second decade, a fine "jam" or "squeeze." Margaret Smith went to a drawing room held in the temporary president's house in early December 1816. "There were not above 200 people, and it was too thin to feel at one's ease. A crowd is certainly animating."[45] Large numbers afforded some protection for the timid. One evening Dolley Madison requested that Margaret Smith's niece play and sing. The young lady declined, and her aunt did not quarrel with the decision. "Had it been a squeeze, I should have urged her playing, but in so thin a room, I knew she would be too conspicuous."[46]

The consequences of these performances were not always those intended. The young ladies in *What Is Gentility?* who anticipated receiving "general attention and admiration" instead were "completely lost in the crowd—and not only my dress but my self too," added one. The daughters of a poor officer and a rich shopkeeper did not have "beauty sufficient to attract attention in a brilliant throng, though they did very well at home."[47] In *The L . . . Family,* the father and son, who are office seekers, initially are delighted when the president receives them graciously and listens to their requests. Later, a more experienced acquaintance laughs and asks, "Are you so ignorant of the language of Courts, as to take what the President, out of politeness has said, for an assurance that you will be successful?"[48] Like all people, the fictional characters had to learn some realities about themselves and the world.

Whether the White House drawing rooms brought personal success or disappointment, they suited the social needs of the people and their government. William Wirt, the Virginia lawyer and author who was in Washington in 1815, two years before he began a twelve-year stretch as attorney general, wrote to his wife that he would attend one of Mrs. Madison's drawing rooms: "it is a show and I get it without paying for it."[49] He must have forgotten that the show of a presidential drawing room was his very own, "a strange compound of almost all nations and ranks" brought together "by motives as various as the characters they possess."[50]

ANNUAL RECEPTIONS

The presence of the general populace and a merry, festive atmosphere characterized the two annual White House receptions. On these occasions the people not only greeted their presidents but also celebrated their nation. In the summer they remembered its birth, and as the year turned they looked forward to its continuing good fortune. As the *National Intelligencer* reported after the 1805 celebration, "There prevailed throughout the company a lively joy at the return of another year, crowned with it the continued enjoyment of peace, liberty and prosperity."

After the term *levee* no longer so clearly indicated an evening open house, it was retained for the custom of paying the compliments of New Year's Day and the Fourth of July to the president and his family in the "morning," defined socially as between noon and two o'clock.[51] More than the time of day distinguished the two types of events. According to a character in one of the novels, drawing rooms were "mere conversation parties, where men talk, often without sitting, and mostly by snatches." However, for the "President's levee . . . a fine band of music [heightens] the pleasure of the scene, and [gives] a zest to the 'feast of reason and the flow of soul.'"[52] The five novels and the historical records have more to say about receptions on New Year's Day than on the Fourth of July.[53] "Most of the strangers leave Washington shortly after congress adjourns," notes E. Cooley. Permanent residents who could afford to travel or had second homes escaped the heat of a Washington summer by traveling to summer houses or to the newly developing resorts. Both numbers attending and brilliance of appearance seem to have been greater in January than in July.

Senator Samuel Mitchill from New York arrived late for the "great parade" on New Year's Day 1802. Thomas Jefferson stood in the withdrawing room "to salute and converse with visitors. The male part of them walked about or made groups for conversation, while the ladies received the bows and adorations of the gentlemen."[54] When Manesseh Cutler, a Congregational clergyman and congressional representative, went to the 1804 reception, he observed that wine, punch in silver urns, and cake were served. The next year he added the terse note "mammoth cheese" to the refreshment list.[55] In 1809 Catharine Mitchill expanded at length on her husband's earlier description. After commenting on the crowd, the president's greeting, and the refreshments, she told how she and her husband amused themselves "by walking about from room to room," listening to a band that "played at intervals martial, patriotic, & enlivening airs which reverberated through the spacious dome," and "chatting with our old acquaintances and forming new ones." They also looked at the "Indian natives. . . . The faces of these Savages were painted a bright vermillion colour, their heads ornamented with feathers, and their ears and noses adorned with rings."[56]

When commentators referred to mobs coming to the White House, they usually wrote about these national festivals. Visiting Jefferson on January 1, 1804, Louisa Catherine Adams was displeased to find "an unruly crowd of indiscriminate persons from every Class."[57] Although a fictional lady admits to her preference for "the splendour of a court, to such a rabble, as collect at the president's house, on the first of January and the fourth of

July," she acknowledges that her view is a political crime.[58] On another occasion she laughs at the crowd with "their *outré* garments and awkward manners," but her companions parry "her ridicule with their good nature" and more republican praise of their "country, and its government, whose institutions gave such freedom, equality, and happiness, to its citizens."[59] During the early decades of the nineteenth century the elite seem to have had little to complain about. "The *mob*, as some of our aristocratical citizens have denominated the *people*, who on these occasions, were admitted into the president's house, always respectfully opened their ranks, to make way for the guests, as they passed into the drawing-room."[60]

In spite of the comments of Louisa Catherine Adams and others, people who enjoyed the festival of a New Year's Day levee sorted literally into insiders and outsiders, distinctions clarified in the novel *A Winter in Washington.* A child and her nurse watch a procession of carriages heading to the White House. After that splendor had passed, they were still amply amused as "various groups of men, women, and children, black and white" dressed in their best clothes made "their way to the president's square." The "mingled population . . . on that day, as well as the fourth of July, crowded to see, not simply the president, but see the *quality* and their fine carriages." Inside there was some mixup of company, as one polished regular told a fine newcomer, "You will die with laughing . . . to see what odd figures, odd dresses, awkward bows, scrapings, and courtesies, are exhibited on these occasions. . . . I will tell you who and who such and such a *nobody* is; for you will not see above fifty or sixty *somebodies*, at most; the rest is a motley crowd, made up of all sorts of folks, that no one ever sees on other occasions."[61]

Basil Hall, a British traveler, attended the New Year's Day levee of 1828 and wittily tried to figure out the method of separating outsiders from insiders. "On the 4th of July . . . all the world attends; but on New Year's day there is some principle of exclusion exercised. How this matter is effected in practice I could never find out, but I can imagine the poor porter

BARBARA G. CARSON

Elizabeth Kortright Monroe, attributed to John Vanderlyn, 1816 or 1820. Invariably elegant, Mrs. James Monroe chose an ermine scarf to complement her black velvet Empire-style gown for this portrait. Although she had gone abroad with her husband on diplomatic missions, delicate health limited her activities and enjoyment in her eight years as First Lady.

to have a delicate job of it; for, in a land of universal equality, the line of admission must often lie so close to that of exclusion, that to split the difference may require fine tools."[62]

Curiously, throughout the early nineteenth century this day of the motley crowd was also the day the quality chose to present their daughters to society. In 1802 Samuel Mitchill commented that "several belles from Virginia and elsewhere were brought out on this gala day."[63] The fictional family in *A Winter in Washington* introduced their daughter at a New Year's reception.[64] The practice was observed as late as 1818. Rosalie Stier, a wealthy Belgian who married George Calvert, a planter descendant of Maryland's founding family, and lived at Riverside just to the northeast of Washington, described her daughter Caroline's entry into society. "The first time she appeared was New Year's Day where we went to the President's House in the morning. Everyone goes there on that day."[65] Rosalie Calvert did not extend the meaning of "everyone" to include "all people." By "everyone" she meant the nobodies among the insiders.

The anticipation and ambience of these events created lasting impressions on visitors. Most had little to say about the visual impact of architecture or furnishings. Instead, they concentrated on "fine dress and beauty," which furnished "the theme of conversation for the following day."[66] Perhaps this was because the people who came from all over the United States and "from most parts of christendom" were "so tenacious of their own fashions" that they created a situation in Washington where dress was "less uniform than in any other fashionable place in the United States."[67] Gentlemen had to make a "genteel and fashionable appearance," but their anxiety about dress meant choosing between boots and shoes or avoiding the exchange or loss of hats and cloaks left in the antechamber.[68] The appearance of the plainly clothed president and most other male guests contrasted with the plumage of foreign ministers, Native Americans, U.S. military officers, and even members of the Marine Band, who wore scarlet uniforms faced and edged in blue.[69] A fictional character observed one

French minister with his "display of gold lace, tinsel, and embroidery." Juliana Seaton saw him as "a rolling ball of burnished gold, carried with swiftness through the air by two gilt wings."[70] The ball was the minister, and his wings "gorgeous footmen with *chapeaux bas,* gilt braided skirts and splendid swords." Then there was the special envoy from Tunis, Sidi Suleyman Mellimelni, who arrived "in the Turkish costume, of the richest materials . . . a kind of robe, or tunic, fell back, and discovered beneath a scarlet doublet, or jacket, splendidly embroidered with gold, with buttons of precious stones."[71]

For ladies, daytime levees did not require the same finery as evening drawing rooms. Still, there were no simple solutions for selecting fabric, color, cut, and trimmings. The Calvert women appeared in dresses and hats from Europe. When Rosalie thanked her sister, she reported competitively that "Mrs. Monroe, her daughters, and four or five other Washington women receive their clothes from Paris, but they are not in as good taste as ours."[72] Those who bought locally, like the ladies in *Winter in Washington,* debated "loveliness adorned" or whether a "cottage bonnet" with flowers and one made of black velvet would do for the occasion. Their fashionable relative had bought a Spanish hat, "turned up in front and shaded with a plume of feathers," for her "magazine of female paraphernalia."[73]

Turbans were à la mode with full ball dress for evenings. The fictional Mrs. L wore her "fine changeable silk, which she had bought at New York."[74] Other ladies at the same party "were dressed with various tastes, and some indeed, scarcely dressed at all, for their bosoms and necks were almost entirely bare . . . a display of Indian style."[75] Seeing exposed flesh gave some a moral jolt; others worried about catching colds. The ladies, real and imagined, dressed as best they could. They then took the arms of their escorts, and all participated in a national celebration.

Belles, buffoons, pretty ladies, and politicians all came to Washington. They did not necessarily rub shoulders with each other at the President's House. In the early national period, as today, equality was more a dream

A line at a New Year's Day reception, ca. 1905. The north door was still the entrance for this largest of the annual public receptions, which was held at the White House until 1933. Steeped in a century of tradition, the President's House inevitably had taken on a widespread and powerful meaning for the American people.

than a reality. The Jackson inauguration, which came after the five novels were published, was the first occasion when "all the world" felt a measure of social entitlement hinted at in the concept of political equality. The historical figures and the fictional characters introduced here had diverse experiences in Washington at the President's House. The delicate instru-

BARBARA G. CARSON

ments of social division—dress, deportment, ambition, and confidence—separated the larger body of the sovereign people into the fashionable and the traditional, somebodies and nobodies, and insiders and outsiders. Nevertheless, each citizen, from his or her vantage point, saw the White House and the events there as personally meaningful and nationally symbolic. "What kind of a government is that of the United States?" asks a fictional character. Another replies, "It is one, sir . . . which you neither feel nor see."[76] A nonvisible, nontangible government needed to assure its people it was real. During these early national years the White House became the solid focus of a bundle of abstract beliefs and cherished hopes. As James Monroe wrote in 1818, "For a building so extensive, intended for a purpose exclusively national . . . a mingled regard is due to the simplicity and purity of our institutions, and to the character of the people."[77]

NOTES

1. E. Cooley, *A Description of the Etiquette at Washington City* (Philadelphia: L. B. Clarke, 1829), 77.

2. For clarity, *levee* will indicate either of these annual midday receptions, and *drawing room* the evening parties scheduled regularly during congressional sessions. Originally associated with the ceremonial morning dressing of a European head of state who needed to be accessible to citizens or subjects of the realm, the term *levee* was more widely and less precisely applied in the eighteenth and nineteenth centuries to official receptions held at any hour and to the practice of wealthy persons receiving visitors and conducting business in bedchambers. In America in both the colonial and early national periods, it seems limited to official events. On the other hand, *drawing room* was applied to private as well as government-hosted events. See Graham Hood, *The Governor's Palace in Williamsburg* (Williamsburg, Va.: The Colonial Williamsburg Foundation, 1991), 108–10.

3. Margaret Bayard Smith, *A Winter in Washington; or, Memoirs of the Seymour Family* (New York: E. Bliss and E. White, 1824) and *What Is Gentility?* (Washington: Pishey Thompson, 1828); [George Watterston], *Wanderer in Washington* (Washington: J. Elliot, Jr., 1827) and *The L . . . Family at Washington; or, A Winter in the Metropolis* (Washington: Davis and Force, 1822); Harry Nimrod, "editor," *The Fudge Family in Washington* (Baltimore: Joseph Robinson, 1820).

SOCIAL SEASONS

4. Smith, *Winter in Washington,* 1:vii–viii. In addition to her two published novels, Smith wrote two more, "Julia" and "Lucy," which remain in manuscript in the William Thornton Papers, Library of Congress. She also privately printed a short children's story, "Diversions of Sidney" (1805).

5. Smith, *What Is Gentility?,* introduction and p. 140.

6. W. W. Abbot, ed., *The Papers of George Washington, April–June 1789,* Presidential Series 2 (Charlottesville: University Press of Virginia, 1978), 248.

7. Dumas Malone, "Without Benefit of Protocol: The Merry Affair," in *Jefferson the President: First Term, 1801–1805* (Boston: Little, Brown, 1970), 367–92.

8. Barbara G. Carson, *Ambitious Appetites: Dining, Behavior and Patterns of Consumption in Federal Washington* (Washington: The American Institute of Architects Press, 1990), 158–61, 205.

9. At the Octagon, 18th Street and New York Avenue, from November 1814 to March 1815, and then in a row-house complex called the Seven Buildings at 19th Street and Pennsylvania Avenue.

10. Cooley, *Description of the Etiquette,* 84–99.

11. Ibid., 5–14. The author comments on the uniqueness of some forms of etiquette in Washington (p. 24) and on the "ease and freedom" of behavior that includes women (p. 70).

12. This brief summary is based on several works: William Seale, *The President's House: A History* (Washington: White House Historical Association, 1986) and *The White House: The History of an American Idea* (Washington: American Institute of Architects Press, 1992); DAR Museum, Washington, D.C., "Magnificent Intentions: Decorative Arts of the District of Columbia, 1791–1861" (1992); The Octagon, Washington, D.C., "In the Most Fashionable Style: Making a Home in the Federal City" (1992); Ellen Kirven Donald, "Household Furnishings in Early Washington, DC," (unpublished manuscript, The Octagon, 1992).

13. Latrobe Letter Book, November 29, 1810, pp. 664–65, quoted in Donald, "Household Furnishings," chap. 8, p. 12.

14. Harrison Gray Otis, January 30, 1818, Harrison Gray Otis Papers, Massachusetts Historical Society, Boston (hereafter Otis Papers).

15. *The Diary of Elbridge Gerry, Jr.,* ed. Claude G. Bowers (New York: Brentano's, 1927), 131.

16. Nimrod, *The Fudge Family,* 39, 40, 43.

17. The White House Collection. Probably to Theodorus Bailey, congressman from New York. See Carson, *Ambitious Appetites,* 154.

18. References to the dinner parties, both given during the Monroe administra-

tion, are in Nimrod, *The Fudge Family*, 38–43, and Watterston, *Wanderer in Washington*, 150–53.

19. Carson, *Ambitious Appetites*, 86–92.

20. Ibid., 114 and 196n36.

21. Watterston, *Wanderer*, 151.

22. Carson. *Ambitious Appetites*, 95.

23. This is especially evident in Margaret Bayard Smith's unpublished novels, "Julia" and "Lucy." See Barbara G. Carson, Ellen Kirven Donald, and Kym S. Rice, "Household Encounters: Servants, Slaves, and Mistresses in Early Washington" (forthcoming in volume of Winterthur Conference, 1992).

24. Nimrod, "The Fudge Family," 39.

25. Watterston, *Wanderer*, 57–58.

26. Ibid., 150; Cooley, *Description of Etiquette*, 5–6.

27. Watterston, *Wanderer*, 76.

28. Cooley, *Description of Etiquette*, 11.

29. Carson, *Ambitious Appetites*, 160–61. Another guest added ice cream to the list in 1809. The cakes may have been a heavy fruitcake or a lighter, sweet sponge cake.

30. Cooley, *Description of Etiquette*, 9.

31. Smith, *What Is Gentility?*, 150.

32. William Stebbins. *The Journal of William Stebbins: Stratford to Washington in 1810* (Conn.: The Acorn Club, 1968), 41.

33. Cooley, *Description of Etiquette*, 83.

34. Cooley further clarifies the procedure: "Strangers not particularly distinguished are introduced to [the president] at his levees" (*Description of the Etiquette*, 4; see also 6, 14–15, and 31–33).

35. Carson, *Ambitious Appetites*, 161n69.

36. Watterston, *Wanderer*, 76.

37. Marilyn Kay Parr, "Augustus John Foster and the 'Washington Wilderness': Personal Letters of a British Diplomat" (Ph.D. diss., George Washington University, 1987), 220.

38. Smith, *What Is Gentility?*, 126–29, 138–59.

39. Watterston, *Wanderer*, 61–62.

40. Louisa Catherine Adams, "The Adventures of Nobody," Adams Family Papers, Massachusetts Historical Society, Boston, p. 216.

41. Diary of Harriet Otis, Otis Papers, February 1812 "Thursday 13th," p. 41.

42. Harrison Gray Otis to Sally Foster Otis, January 7, 1821, Otis Papers. The hostess was Mrs. Joseph Gale.

43. Catharine Mitchill to Margaret Akerly Miller, February 21, 1812, Mitchill Papers, Library of Congress.

44. Carson, *Ambitious Appetites*, 161.

45. Margaret Bayard Smith, *The First Forty Years of Washington Society, Portrayed by the Family Letters of Mrs. Samuel Harrison Smith*, ed. Gaillard Hunt (New York: Scribner's, 1906), 130. Crowds tended to be thin early and late in the season or when people, especially women, boycotted events for their own social reasons. For instance, after Elizabeth Monroe announced she would not make calls, the Washington ladies refused to attend her drawing room (Carson, *Ambitious Appetites*, 162–63).

46. Ibid., 132.

47. Smith, *What Is Gentility?*, 158.

48. Watterston, *The L . . . Family*, 123.

49. Carson, *Ambitious Appetites*, 161.

50. Watterston, *Wanderer*, 56.

51. Cooley, *Description of the Etiquette*, 80.

52. Watterston, *The L . . . Family*, 126. See Elise K. Kirk, *Music at the White House: A History of the American Spirit* (Urbana: University of Illinois Press, 1986), 7–48.

53. The best fictional description of a July Fourth reception is in M. B. Smith, *Winter in Washington* (London: H. K. Newman, 1824), 215–17.

54. Carson, *Ambitious Appetites*, 155.

55. Ibid. The presentation of a cheese as large as a millstone generated much publicity at the New Year's Day reception of 1802. It was the gift of the people of Cheshire, a town in western Massachusetts. Jefferson ordered a special table to display it, and guests gradually consumed it over several years. See C. Ca. Browne, "Elder John Leland and the Mammoth Cheshire Cheese," *Agricultural History* 18 (October 1944):145–53; Lyman H. Butterfield, "Elder John Leland, Jefferson Itinerant," *American Antiquarian Society Proceedings* 62 (1952):214–30; Bernard Mayo, "A Peppercorn for Mr. Jefferson," *Virginia Quarterly Review* 19 (1943):222–35.

56. Carson, *Ambitious Appetites*, 156. On this occasion mainly men and women of the Delaware and Cherokee tribes. The entertainment is described in Smith, *Winter in Washington*, as "inspiriting and animating sound of national airs and military music" (41).

57. Carson, *Ambitious Appetites*, 157.

58. Smith, *Winter in Washington* 1:13.

59. Ibid., 1:52.

BARBARA G. CARSON

60. Ibid., 1:41.

61. Ibid., 1:38–39. See also Cooley, *Description of the Etiquette,* 42–43. The mother in Watterston, *The L . . . Family,* curtsies in the fashion of 1776 (82).

62. Basil Hall, *Travels in North America in the Years 1827 and 1828* (Philadelphia: Carey, Lea & Carey, 1829), 3:13–14.

63. Carson, *Ambitious Appetites,* 155.

64. Smith, *Winter in Washington,* 1:39–64.

65. Margaret Law Callcott, ed., *Mistress of Riversdale: The Plantation Letters of Rosalie Stier Calvert, 1795–1821* (Baltimore: Johns Hopkins University Press, 1991), 330–31.

66. Cooley, *Description of the Etiquette,* 13.

67. Ibid., 64–65.

68. Ibid., 61. Elsewhere (12) Cooley states that many gentlemen wore boots rather than shoes to the president's levees because there was no dancing on these occasions.

69. Smith, *Winter in Washington* 1:40, and Kirk, *Music at the White House,* 22.

70. Smith, *Winter in Washington* 1:49–50, and Carson, *Ambitious Appetites,* 95.

71. Smith, *Winter in Washington* 1:49–50. Mellimelni was negotiating the return of three ships captured by the United States during its war with Tripoli.

72. Callcott, *Mistress of Riversdale,* 348.

73. Smith, *Winter in Washington* 1:12, 17, 27, 28.

74. Watterston, *The L . . . Family,* 81.

75. Ibid., 86.

76. Smith, *Winter in Washington* 2:180.

77. Lee, Bill of Appropriations, request for furnishing fund, February 1818, quoted in Donald, "Household Furnishings in Early Washington, DC," chap. 8, p. 23.

— FOUR —

Decorated in the Most Splendid Manner: Art in the White House

WILLIAM KLOSS

THE WHITE HOUSE art collection is wide in scope, diverse in subject matter, style, and national range. It is primarily American and encompasses portraiture, landscape, genre, still life, and historical subjects; neoclassical, romantic, and realistic styles; art from the East, the West, the South, and the Midwest; and depictions of the city, the country, and the frontier. This art has come into the White House by design, with its significance for the President's House firmly in mind. Since it reflects the history and inhabitants of the house, it is unlike any other collection in the capital city.

The title of this essay is taken from a letter of December 17, 1819, by Samuel F. B. Morse, subsequently the inventor of the telegraph, who at that moment was painting the portrait of President Monroe. He wrote,

> Wednesday evening Mrs. Monroe held a drawing-room. I attended
> and made my bow. She was splendidly and tastily dressed. The
> drawing-room and suite of rooms at the President's are furnished

and decorated in the most splendid manner; some think too much so, but I do not. Something of splendor is certainly proper about the Chief Magistrate for the credit of the nation. Plainness can be carried to an extreme, and in national buildings and establishments it will, with good reason, be styled meanness.[1]

The portrait of Monroe is a good example of art in the collection that has an intimate connection with the White House, since Morse came to the mansion to paint the president. The life portrait was taken to Charleston, South Carolina, where Morse used it as the basis of a full-length portrait commissioned by that city. The president greatly admired the life portrait, as did one of his daughters, who requested a replica from the artist. Our painting, descended in the Monroe family, is presumed to be that replica.[2]

Henry Inman's regal and sensuous portrait of Angelica Singleton Van Buren (1842) was painted one year after President Martin Van Buren's term had ended. But it accurately reflects the love of elegance in attitude and clothing that marked the character of his daughter-in-law, who served as White House hostess during the widower president's administration. Moreover, the bust of Van Buren that was carved by Hiram Powers at the outset of the presidency, and that is now in the same room with this portrait, was included in the picture by Inman.

Portraits understandably dominate the White House collection, but landscape plays a major role as well. One of the finest examples, in which a genre subject is set into a landscape, is George Caleb Bingham's *Lighter Relieving a Steamboat Aground* (1847). It is a precious record of the frontier when that was marked by the Missouri and Mississippi rivers. It has a political subtext, for the Democratic president James K. Polk had recently vetoed a River and Harbor Bill that would have provided for clearing snags and shoals such as that upon which the distant steamer has run; Bingham was an active Whig supporter of the bill. It is a deeply nostalgic picture, conjuring up an earlier date before such rafts were greatly outnumbered by steamboats.

James Monroe, painted by Samuel F. B. Morse, ca. 1819. Morse has idealized the president, whose administrations earned the sobriquet "the era of good feeling." The genesis of this portrait was a commission for a full-length portrait from the City of Charleston, South Carolina. This forcefully painted bust-length portrait was a replica done for Monroe's daughter and it reflects the combination of formality and zest, elegance and liveliness, also characteristic of the Monroe White House. Morse commented on the rebuilt and newly decorated rooms of the President's House: "The drawing-room and the suite of rooms at the President's are furnished and decorated in the most splendid manner; some think too much so, but I do not. . . . Plainness can be carried to an extreme."

Another landscape with a message, but of a very different sort, is Asher B. Durand's *The Indian's Vespers* (1847). This is one of the finest paintings by America's first major native-born landscape artist. When it was received by the White House in 1963 it bore the fanciful title "The Last of the Mohicans," but it has nothing to do with Fenimore Cooper's novel. It was commissioned by the American Art-Union, the major patron of American artists during the 1840s, which issued engravings of commissioned works to all its members and distributed the original paintings by lottery. The

WILLIAM KLOSS

subject of Durand's painting was specifically left to his own choice, and it was misunderstood by contemporary critics. They correctly observed that the artist had depicted morning light at the left and the setting sun at the right, but saw it as a willful distortion of nature: "We would rather see one touch of nature than so much of Durand."[3] The critics were too literal-minded. The painting is a transcendental symbol of life's brief course and of the passage from the uncleared forests of life to the redemption of eternal

Lighter Relieving a Steamboat Aground, painted by George Caleb Bingham, 1847. This painting brings to life an era and a region in which storytelling was a way of life and an art form. Bingham has depicted an accident on the river: the steamboat in the distance has run aground on a shoal. But the artist's primary focus is on the monumental group of self-sufficient, idle boatmen, his heroes, interlocked figures fixed in place by the artist's customary geometry of a pyramid and carefully aligned with the picture plane, raptly listening to their storyteller after having removed ("lightened") cargo from the steamer.

The Indian's Vespers, painted by Asher B. Durand, 1847. With this painting Durand made a major statement in theme as well as size, recombining nature's elements in a grand, symbolic canvas. The recurrent belief in the immanence of God in nature was given emphasis in America through the writings of Ralph Waldo Emerson. The Indian, his arms raised to the sun in praise, is bathed in light. Ambitiously and reverently, Durand has summoned virgin forests, vast waters, insubstantial mists, man in his natural state, and the sun's unifying eye to evoke the ancient roots and yearnings of mankind.

WILLIAM KLOSS

light. It closely parallels a passage in Ralph Waldo Emerson's "Nature," an essay reissued to wide public acclaim in 1847, the year of this painting. Emerson wrote: "In the woods, we return to reason and faith. . . . Standing on the bare ground—my head bathed by the blithe air and uplifted into infinite space—all mean egotism vanishes. I become a transparent eyeball; I am nothing; I see all; the currents of the Universal Being circulate through me; I am part or parcel of God."[4]

Some works of art in the White House are an integral part both of the history of the house and of the nation. Foremost among these is Gilbert Stuart's *George Washington* (1797). One of four versions of the so-called Lansdowne type, its attribution has sometimes been doubted—partly because of a certain weakness of drawing (for example, in the head of Washington) and partly because Stuart pointedly denied having painted it. He had reason to do so, for the always improvident artist had sold the painting twice. It was commissioned by Charles Cotesworth Pinckney, minister designate to France, for display in the embassy there. Pinckney's credentials were not accepted, and the painting, though paid for, was not delivered. Stuart sold it again to the proprietor of a popular New York museum, at whose death it passed to a creditor who sold it in 1800 to the U.S. government for the adornment of the White House. Since Pinckney, in correspondence, repeatedly pressed Stuart to deliver the painting, it is hardly surprising that on the artist's visit to Washington two years later he insisted that he had not painted it.

The portrait, a rich amalgam of the symbols of presidential authority in a democratic society, has been in the White House since the doors opened, except for its dramatic removal before the mansion was burned by the British in August 1814 during the War of 1812. In a famous act, Dolley Madison enlisted two passersby to break the frame of the life-size portrait

Facing page: George Washington, painted by Gilbert Stuart, 1797. Stuart's authoritative image of the first president, with his right arm extended in one of the ancient Roman oratorical gestures, conveys the unyielding resolve and severe dignity that made him the embodiment of the young Republic. Dolley Madison was determined to keep this full-length portrait, in addition to official papers, out of British hands when troops set fire to the President's House in August 1814. The painting was carried into the safety of the countryside, and not returned to the rebuilt White House until 1817.

and carry the painting on its stretcher to safety in the countryside. It returned to the reconstructed house in 1817.

Also in 1817, three marble busts entered the Monroe White House. Carved around 1815 in Italy from terracotta models made by Giuseppe Ceracchi more than twenty years before, they represented Amerigo Vespucci, Christopher Columbus, and George Washington. In the early 1790s Ceracchi had twice visited America, where he modeled numerous portraits. Back in Europe, his ardent republicanism led him to plot the assassination of Napoleon, a failed attempt that resulted in his execution in 1801. The three busts in the White House were purchased from Benjamin Lear, son of Tobias Lear. The elder Lear had been Washington's secretary and subsequently consul at Algiers. After his recall, he had become active in the importation of sculpture from an American agent at Livorno, from whom he ordered these three examples. Upon his demise, his son completed the transaction with the government.

In 1821–22 President Monroe received a delegation of Indian leaders at the White House. Their portraits, including that of Monchousia (White Plume), of the Kansa tribe, were painted at that time by Charles Bird King, mostly on government commission. The vast majority of the more than two hundred such portraits by King were destroyed in a fire in the Smithsonian Building in 1865, rendering the five now in the White House especially precious.

Stuart's portraits of John Quincy Adams and his wife Louisa Catherine Johnson Adams came into the White House collection in 1971, gifts of their descendants. The likeness of Mrs. Adams was begun in 1821 when Adams was secretary of state but not completed until 1826, during his presidency. It was not a happy time for his wife. "Next," wrote her grandson, Henry Adams, "she lived four miserable years in the White House."[5] The portrait accurately reflects her experience. In 1827 she wrote:

> I saw my portrait at the exhibition. John and Jane were perfectly horrified. Nobody likes it and Stewart is quite vexed. It looks very much as I looked, like a woman who was just attacked by the first chill of death and the features stiffning into torpor. . . . It speaks too much of inward suffering and a half broken heart to be an agreeable remembrancer. Mais n'import—'tis but a speaking tell tale which may in time of need long after I am gone . . . give a lesson both of feeling and wisdom.[6]

Landscape, as we have seen, can carry extrapictorial meaning, and George Cooke's *City of Washington from beyond the Navy Yard* (1833)

Amerigo Vespucci, modeled in terra-cotta by Giuseppe Ceracchi, ca. 1790–94; carved in marble ca. 1815. Although his voyages of 1499 and 1501 were preceded by those of Columbus, only Vespucci realized that he had "arrived at a new land which . . . we observed to be a continent." Early in 1791 the Italian-born Ceracchi, noted sculptor and ardent republican, arrived in Philadelphia, where he hoped to receive a congressional commission. Although the Florentine Ceracchi returned to Europe in 1792, the politically engaged artist continued to carve busts of a number of the Founding Fathers as well as Columbus and Vespucci, which were sent to patrons in America.

Louisa Catherine Johnson Adams, painted by Gilbert Stuart, 1821–26. This penetrating image of a sorrowful Mrs. John Quincy Adams epitomizes the high achievement of the last years of Stuart's career. The artist, notorious for unconscionable delays, took five years to complete this painting. As the wife of the secretary of state, Louisa Catherine Adams had been relatively happy; but as First Lady, "she lived four miserable years in the White House," as her grandson Henry Adams put it plainly. When she saw the finished portrait at the Boston Athenaeum in 1827, she wrote: "It speaks too much of inward suffering and a half broken heart to be an agreeable remembrancer."

ART IN THE WHITE HOUSE

City of Washington from beyond the Navy Yard, painted by George Cooke, 1833. Two large dry docks flank a three-masted schooner at the Navy shipyard on the Anacostia River below the Capitol. This grouping serves as a strong base for Capitol Hill and the Capitol Building as it appeared in 1833 with the dome designed by Charles Bulfinch. The view is balanced by the White House in the distance at left center. Between these two buildings the city lies on lower ground, composed of town houses and steepled churches. To the left is the confluence of the Anacostia and the Potomac River, whose broad waters stretch to the port of Georgetown.

surely does so. A glance reveals that Cooke has enlarged the White House at left center so that it exactly balances the nearer Capitol at right center, and has set both within a radiant and peaceful landscape. In this straightforward way the artist conveys the balance of the executive and the legislative, and the harmony of democratic government.

WILLIAM KLOSS

The disruption of that harmony in Civil War and its subsequent hopeful restoration are reflected in a number of works of art in the White House. For instance, Thomas Nast in *Hungry Office Seakers* shows us the scene in the lobby of Willard's Hotel on March 6, 1861, two days after Lincoln's inauguration. The president elect had been staying at Willard's (not the present hotel, but its predecessor on the same site), quite near the White

Hungry Office Seekers, pencil, ink, and wash on paper by Thomas Nast, 1861. This delightful sketch is a scene in Willard's, Washington's leading hotel just two blocks from the White House, two days after the inauguration of Abraham Lincoln. It was there that Lincoln stayed and spent most of his time during the pre-inauguration week. A historian of the city has written: "Willard's held an unprecedented collection of men notable in public affairs, civil, military and naval. Republican leaders were there to confer, and delegations to press their advice. . . . Past the new President, from early morning until late at night, streamed minor politicians, place seekers, editors, reporters and handshakers." Thomas Nast would later become famous, as an illustrator, for his crusade against the notorious Tweed Ring of politicians who defrauded New York City.

House. The twenty-year-old Nast had been sent to Washington to prepare drawings for the *New York Illustrated News*. An extraordinary congregation of persons could be found staying here, or meeting here, or just being seen here. Even at the end of March, as a contemporary diarist wrote, "There are men at Willard's who have come literally thousands of miles to seek for places which can only be theirs for four years."[7] Some of the men in this drawing are identified or identifiable. At right center, with his trademark throat whiskers, is Horace Greeley, the famous antislavery editor of the *New York Tribune*. The tall man at far left was a famous pugilist, later congressman, John Morrissey, who shakes hands with Frank Leslie, editor of *Frank Leslie's Illustrated Newspaper*.

In 1864 President Lincoln received the gift of a painting from a group of New England abolitionists and their spokesman, William Lloyd Garrison. It was William Tolman Carlton's *Watch Meeting—Dec. 31st 1862—Waiting for the Hour* (1863) and it depicted a congregation of slaves moments before the Emancipation Proclamation took effect. Somber and passionately felt, the painting apparently left the White House with the widowed Mary Todd Lincoln. The artist's oil study for the painting filled its place in 1976 and today hangs in the Lincoln Bedroom, which in 1863 was Lincoln's office.

In late March 1865 Lincoln sailed to City Point, on the James River, aboard the presidential steamer. There, with generals Grant and Sherman and Admiral Porter, he discussed peace terms to be offered to the Confederacy as the war appeared near an end. In his second Inaugural Address, Lincoln had already enunciated his own attitude: "With malice toward none; with charity for all." George P. A. Healy recreated this meeting in *The Peacemakers* (1868). It is a still, somber painting, despite the forceful gesture of Sherman. Healy, painting with the knowledge of subsequent events, imbued his figures and the setting with symbolic significance. Petersburg had fallen on April 2, and on the fourth Lincoln walked in undefended Richmond. The end of the terrible war receives acknowledgment in the rainbow behind Lincoln. Of course it signifies the advent of peace, but its profounder meaning comes from the biblical account of God's covenant with man after the flood (Genesis 8–9):

> I will not again curse the ground any more for man's sake; . . . neither will I again smite any more every thing living, as I have done. . . . This is the token of the covenant which I make between me and you and every living creature that is with you, for perpetual generations: I do set my [rain]bow in the cloud, and it shall be for a token of a covenant between me and the earth. . . . And I will remember my covenant, . . . and the waters shall no more become a flood to destroy all flesh.

The year after Healy painted *The Peacemakers* he had the inspiration to paint the president alone, in basically the same pose. Where before Lincoln had listened to his military leaders, now he seemed to listen to distant voices. It was a profoundly appropriate way to commemorate the fallen leader. Given to the White House by the widow of Robert Todd Lincoln, the president's son, the painting hangs today in the State Dining Room.

When the Civil War had ended and President Grant had gained the White House, a redecoration of the Entrance Hall introduced a rousingly patriotic scheme in red, white, and blue, with portraits of Washington and Lincoln, and in the ceiling two allegorical figures by the Italian-born Constantino Brumidi, who had just completed his monumental fresco in the new dome of the U.S. Capitol. Female figures personifying *Liberty* and *Union* (1869) soared above the viewer's head bearing or accompanied by the appropriate symbolic attributes.

A memorable seascape by Martin Johnson Heade, *Sailing Off the Coast* (1869), is also probably a comment on the outcome of the Civil War. The solemn ship, majestic and serene on the calm sea, seems an echo of Long-

Sailing Off the Coast, painted by Martin Johnson Heade, 1869. Heade's romantic coastal reverie, devoid of human observers, gives a disconsolate sense of time passing irrevocably. This sense is established by the measured recession of the silent sails toward the sunset horizon, by the numberless pink and blue-gray bands of light and shadow that form the surface of the ocean, and by the pale pink-bellied clouds that hover almost regretfully above the horizon while the day holds its breath before expiring. The mood of this painting of an unidentified shoreline (perhaps Newport) is the mood of the country after the Civil War.

fellow's ringing prewar exhortation: "Sail on, O Ship of State! Sail on, O Union, strong and great!"

At the end of the century another, lesser, war had briefly preoccupied the nation. The Spanish-American War (that "splendid little war," said John Hay) established the United States as a naval power and, with longer consequences, as a colonial power. The conclusion of the war is the subject of Théobald Chartran's *Signing of the Peace Protocol between Spain & United States, August 12, 1898* (1899). The ceremony took place in the White House. President McKinley dominates the scene, standing at the end of the cabinet table in a second-floor room on the south side of the house. The signatories were Secretary of State William Day and, acting for the Spanish, French ambassador Jules Cambon. Chartran used photographs of the event in preparing his canvas. He edited them by reducing the number of participants and by shifting the cabinet table (still in the White House and used for every subsequent treaty signed there) nearer the window to justify his lighting scheme.

Just four years later John Singer Sargent painted President Theodore Roosevelt on the main staircase in the recently remodeled White House. Roosevelt greatly liked the portrait, but his acerbic neighbor on Lafayette Square, Henry Adams, wrote: "The portrait is good Sargent and not very bad Roosevelt. It is not Theodore, but a young intellectual idealist with a taste for athletics, which I take to be Theodore's idea of himself. It is for once less brutal than its subject. . . . Of course we all approve it."[8]

As the 1914 war in Europe and American involvement in it both grew in intensity, Childe Hassam began a series of paintings of flags on Fifth Avenue, which he continued to develop through the Armistice. His *Avenue in the Rain* is pointedly dated twice: February 1917. The insistent dating calls attention to the exact moment when American patriotic fervor peaked. In little over a month the U.S. entered the war in Europe, thus making it in fact the first *world* war.

Although Hassam disagreed, he was often labeled an American impressionist. As it happens, the White House owns a major work by the French denominator of impressionism, Claude Monet. Together with eight remarkable paintings by Paul Cézanne (the gift of a single donor, Charles A. Loeser), *Morning on the Seine* (1897) stands in clear contrast to the bulk of the collection. A 1963 gift of the family of John F. Kennedy in his

Signing of the Peace Protocol between Spain and United States, August 12, 1898,
painted by Théobald Chartran, 1899. The "splendid little war," as John Hay called the
Spanish-American War, was not one of the nation's prouder conflicts, although it was
one of the most popular. Following the explosion and sinking of the U.S.S. *Maine* in
Havana's harbor in February 1898, Congress declared war in April, and in July the war
was over. The armistice gave independence to Cuba, ceded Puerto Rico to the United
States, and permitted American occupation of Manila in the Philippines. The French
government acted on behalf of the Spanish in the preliminary peace protocol; French
ambassador to the United States Jules Cambon is therefore signing the preliminary peace
document in the painting, with the principal United States representative, Secretary of
State William R. Day. The stout figure on the left, President William McKinley, dominates the proceedings.

WILLIAM KLOSS

memory, it is an aptly meditative memorial, with its mysterious dreaminess and sense of time suspended in a medium of sky and water.

The wistful, silent, profoundly inward quality of the Monet finds a sympathetic echo in the portrait that was painted of Patricia Ryan Nixon eighty years later. Henriette Wyeth, daughter of N. C. Wyeth, sister of Andrew Wyeth, wife (now widow) of Peter Hurd—artists all—was an inspired choice to paint Mrs. Nixon four years after the family left the White House. While there were and are different responses to the portrait within the Nixon family, Julie Nixon Eisenhower has carefully reported the sittings in her compelling book about her mother. Henriette Wyeth wrote to Julie: "Your mother has eyes that are like no one else's. The eyes reveal an unusual spirit. They are the eyes of a sixteen-year-old girl—an expression of great sweetness. And, in that expression, occasionally the doors close and the lights go out. For there is a wistfulness in your mother's beauty. . . . She still believes despite injustices."[9]

Certainly, the complex expression set down here is not the whole personality of Patricia Ryan Nixon. Just as certainly the artist has penetrated, feelingly, to the intensely human, resilient core. We may say, as Louisa Adams did of her equally inward portrait by Gilbert Stuart, that "'tis but a speaking tell tale which may in time of need . . . give a lesson both of feeling and wisdom."

WILLIAM KLOSS

The Avenue in the Rain, painted by Childe Hassam, 1917. Hassam was the most prominent of the "Ten American Painters," a group founded in 1898 and strongly influenced by recent French art. Painted at the height of Hassam's powers, *The Avenue in the Rain* is one of some thirty related, intensely patriotic paintings of flag-decorated streets that the artist produced between 1916 and 1919, during and immediately after the First World War. The avenue is Fifth Avenue in New York City, frequently decorated with flags as American sentiment moved inexorably from isolationism toward intervention following the sinking of the British liner *Lusitania* by a German submarine in May 1915.

NOTES

1. Letter, Morse to his mother, December 17, 1819. Published in Edward Lind Morse, ed., *Samuel F. B. Morse: His Letters and Journals,* 2 vols. (Boston: Houghton Mifflin, 1914), 1:226–27.

2. All of the art discussed in this paper is illustrated and fully discussed in my book: William Kloss, *Art in the White House: A Nation's Pride* (Washington: White House Historical Association, 1992). The ideas and facts presented in this paper are presented or documented there. Here I have restricted citations to quotations, excepting poetry, the Bible, and similar works of common culture.

3. *Literary World* 2, no. 38 (October 23, 1847): 277.

4. Ralph Waldo Emerson, "Nature," in *The Selected Writings of Ralph Waldo Emerson* (New York: Modern Library, 1950), 6.

5. Henry Adams, *The Education of Henry Adams* (1918; reprint, Boston: Houghton Mifflin, 1961), 18.

6. Louisa Adams to Mary Hellen, July 23, 1827. Quoted in Andrew Oliver, *Portraits of John Quincy Adams and His Wife* (Cambridge: Harvard University Press, 1970), 85.

7. William Howard Russell, *My Diary North and South* (New York, 1863), 51, quoted in Hermann Warner Williams, Jr., *The Civil War: The Artists' Record* (Boston: Beacon Press, 1961), 223.

8. Henry Adams, *Letters,* ed. Worthington Chauncey Ford (Boston: Houghton Mifflin, 1938), 398.

9. Quoted in Julie Nixon Eisenhower, *Pat Nixon: The Untold Story* (New York: Simon & Schuster, 1986), 461.

FIVE

Furniture and Interiors: Change and Continuity

BETTY C. MONKMAN

HOME, office, place of ceremony—the White House serves many functions. The Residence Act of 1790, which created the District of Columbia, stipulated only that there be "suitable buildings for the accommodation of Congress, and of the President" in the new federal city.[1] The house for the president was built to reflect the vision of George Washington:

> For the President's House, I would design a building which should
> also look forward, but execute no more of it at present than might
> suit the circumstances of this Country when it shall be first wanted.
> A plan comprehending more may be executed at a future period
> when the wealth, population, and importance of it shall stand upon
> much higher ground than they do at present.[2]

It was to be a place for public ceremonies and the procedures of the office of the president as well as a residence for the chief executive. President Washington and those involved in the creation of the President's House gave much consideration to what the building should represent. In attempting to recruit craftsmen from France to work on the building, the commissioners of the District of Columbia declared, "We wish to exhibit a grandeur of conception, a Republican simplicity, and that true Elegance of proportion which corresponds to a tempered freedom excluding Frivolity, the good of little minds."[3]

Similar concerns were expressed by the New York businessman Gouverneur Morris, who bought French tableware for Washington's New York residence. "I think it of very great importance to fix the taste of our Country properly," he wrote to Washington in 1790, "and I think your Example will go so very far in that respect. It is therefore my Wish that every Thing about you should be substantially good and majestically plain, made to endure."[4] The precedents established by Washington for the presidency continue to influence modern holders of the office, and for nearly two hundred years the house Washington envisioned has continued to function as home, office, and ceremonial center. At the end of the twentieth century it has become also a major tourist attraction and the focus of worldwide media attention as a symbol of the presidency and the American government.

There has always been curiosity about and interest in the President's House, its rooms and furnishings. A mid-nineteenth-century guide to the city of Washington mentioned that the President's House was "one of the first objects of interest visited with eager curiosity."[5] Oliver Wolcott, John Adams's secretary of the treasury, observed in 1800 that the house was built "to be looked at by visitors and strangers."[6]

They came to see the president and be introduced to him, to look at the house and its furnishings, and to attend a social event. Certain rooms on the state floor have been open to the public since 1801, and nineteenth-century presidents received visitors at scheduled hours each week. Until 1933 presidents received the public at the annual New Year's Day reception. Comments and descriptions of visitors varied according to their political persuasion or personal taste. An 1856 handbook describing notable sights

Visitors greeted by a White House police officer in the Entrance Hall, 1881. The White House has been open to the public since 1801.

in the city commented that the interior arrangements were "elegant and convenient, well adapted to the various purposes for which the building was designed," but it went on to note that "as the rooms, both public and private, are newly furnished with the coming of every new administration, we deem it unnecessary to trouble the reader with elaborate descriptions."[7] Most visitors could not resist noting either that the house and its contents

FURNITURE AND INTERIORS

were elegant or that there was a worn appearance to the rooms and furnishings. An 1830 account of the house and its interiors stated:

> Some persons, under every administration, have objected to the style of the President's mansion, as bordering on unnecessary state and parade—but we are of a different opinion. It is the house provided by the people for the residence of the Chief magistrate of their choice . . . it hardly equals the seats of many of the nobility and wealthy commoners of England, and bears no comparison with the residences of the petty princes of Germany, or the grand dukes of Italy: it exhibits no rich marbles, fine statues nor costly paintings. It is what the mansion of the head of this republic should be, large enough for public and family purposes, and should be finished and maintained in a style to gratify every wish for convenience and pleasure.[8]

One of the earliest observers, the English traveler Charles William Janson, portrayed the Jefferson White House in 1806: "The president's house is certainly a neat but plain piece of architecture . . . only part of it is furnished; the whole salary of the president would be inadequate to the expence of completing it in a style of suitable elegance."[9] On the occasion of a visit by a delegation of Winnebago Indians to John Quincy Adams in 1828, Chief Hoowaneka exclaimed, "So large and beautiful was the President's House . . . and every article in it . . . that when I entered it I thought I was in heaven."[10]

The house was rebuilt after being burned by the British in 1814, and the East Room was completely furnished for the first time in 1829. A visitor related in 1830 that "there was some old furniture of the former stock" but the "ornaments are sparse and not of high order." He pronounced, "Some of the furniture of the house is elegant, but in general it looks much abused from the crowds of careless visitors. The Lady's parlour may be said to be superbly furnished, but this remark does not extend to many other rooms."[11] William Stoddard, a White House secretary in the Lincoln administration, declared that the house reminded him of an "old and unsuccessful hotel."[12]

Writing of the Lincoln period, the historian Margaret Leech commented that foreign travelers dismissed the mansion as an "ordinary country house, wanting in either taste or splendor." But, she continued, it was "an object

Office seekers waiting in the Entrance Hall to see the president, 1888. The president and his family, guests, appointments, and tourists entered the house through the north door until 1902, when the president and his staff moved to the newly constructed West Wing.

The Blue Parlor.

Main Entrance to East Room.

In the Corridor

Green Room

Red Room.

White House interiors have always been of great interest to the American people. Here a visitor examines the rooms decorated for President Chester Arthur by Louis Comfort Tiffany in 1882.

BETTY C. MONKMAN

of deep interest to Americans."[13] A Washington socialite in the twentieth century compared attending White House functions during the Wilson administration with those at embassies in the city. "Going to the White House was different. We stepped right into . . . history."[14]

Whether it was an appointment, a guest coming for a reception, or a tourist, until 1902 everyone (including the president and his family) entered through the north door into the Entrance Hall, which often had the appearance of a waiting area. The simple decor of the hall, with its plain stuccoed walls and Ionic columns separating the hall from the corridor, was the first look at the house by the visitor. The large columns were screened from the corridor for heating as early as 1837, and in 1853 a large cast-iron screen with glass panels was designed by Thomas U. Walter, the architect of the Capitol. After 1882 visitors were greeted by the vivid red, white, and blue stained-glass screen created by Louis Comfort Tiffany for Chester Arthur, which was broken up and sold at auction in 1902. Today this space reflects the simpler designs of the colonial revival period installed for Theodore Roosevelt by McKim, Mead & White and modified in the Truman renovation of the 1950s.

Constant changes have taken place in the interiors of the White House. While the exterior remained basically unchanged after the addition of the north portico in 1829–30, the interiors have undergone changes with every administration. By the end of the nineteenth century a Washington correspondent pronounced that the White House "has already become too small and too old-fashioned in its construction and arrangement to be the proper home for the President of the United States."[15]

THE OFFICE

Appointments, office seekers, and those wanting to meet the president flocked to the house in the nineteenth century. Visitors, particularly foreign visitors, were surprised and astonished at the openness of the house to the public and the easy accessibility of the president.[16] One Scottish visitor in the 1830s recalled, "We found no guards at the door of the palace."[17]

In the first year of the Civil War, Washington guidebooks relayed the schedules for being received by the president.

> Business calls are received at all times and hours when the President is unengaged. The morning hours are preferred. Special days and evenings are assigned, each season, for calls of respect—one morning and one afternoon a week usually is assigned. Receptions are held during the winter season, generally once a week, between eight and ten o'clock in the evening at which time guests are expected in full dress.[18]

Beginning in the Jackson administration the office visitor ascended the stairs off the Entrance Hall to the second-floor office quarters, where the president and his staff worked and the cabinet met. (Earlier nineteenth-century presidents had their offices on the state floor.) "A single servant ushered us into a plainly, but comfortably furnished, large parlor, at the fireside of which the president was seated," noted a foreign visitor to Jackson's office.[19] Another visitor at the same time recalled the same room, "where everything announces the august simplicity of our government. . . . The center is occupied by a large table completely covered with books, papers, parchments, etc., and seems like a general repository of every thing that may be wanted for reference; while the president is seated at a smaller table near the fireplace, covered with the papers which are the subject of his immediate attention; and which, by their number, admonish the visitor to occupy no more of his time . . . than necessity requires."[20]

These utilitarian spaces at the east end of the second floor would be the center of the presidency until the West Wing was constructed in 1902. In the earliest image of the president's office and cabinet room, which appeared in a 1856 periodical *The United States Magazine* during the Franklin Pierce

President Abraham Lincoln's office and cabinet room was well documented by artists. In this widely circulated print, Lincoln and his cabinet are depicted at the first reading of the Emancipation Proclamation.

administration, the furnishings were a mix of styles often handed down from one administration to the next. They were not considered historic objects associated with the presidency but furnishings to be used; there were no attempts to preserve any items with historical associations until Mrs. Benjamin Harrison began to preserve state china in the late 1880s.[21]

Before the interiors were photographed, the most documented office was that of President Lincoln. The artist Charles Stellwagon sketched Lincoln's office and cabinet room in 1864 and included maps of such war areas as Virginia, Charleston harbor, and Kentucky; details of his office appeared in

From 1866 until 1902 the cabinet met in a second floor room adjacent to the office that had been used by Lincoln. Here President Rutherford B. Hayes and his cabinet meet in the room recently refurbished by President Ulysses S. Grant.

a widely circulated print of Francis B. Carpenter's painting of the first reading of the Emancipation Proclamation before the cabinet. A portrait of Jackson hung over the mantel, and the furnishings were those that had been used in the room for some thirty years. Carpenter lived in the White House while painting this work and sketched details of the office such as the window treatments, the chandelier, and the carpet design.

By 1866 Andrew Johnson had moved the cabinet into the adjoining room to the west, which had been used as a reception and waiting area. Here the cabinet would meet until the West Wing was built. President Grant

BETTY C. MONKMAN

completely refurbished the room in 1869 with furnishings in the fashionable Renaissance Revival style, supplied by the New York firm Pottier and Stymus. A substantial number of these objects survived in the White House to be used throughout the family quarters. In the early twentieth century, presidents such as Theodore Roosevelt, William H. Taft, Woodrow Wilson, and Warren Harding used the old cabinet room as a private office or study and filled it with personal as well as White House objects. It was a space where the president could receive callers more privately than in the new office building, the current West Wing. Today the room is again a private office used by the president.

In the early twentieth century, the old cabinet room was used by the presidents as a private study. President Woodrow Wilson spent considerable time writing speeches, meeting with aides, and taking care of his correspondence in this room.

FURNITURE AND INTERIORS

THE HOME

The family quarters have always been the most personal areas of the White House, a space where families have made a public building their home and led private lives away from the demands of office and public ceremony. Mrs. William H. Taft wrote that she was "always conscious of the character which a century of history had impressed upon the White House" but noted that "it came to feel as much like home as any house I have ever occupied."[22]

An earlier First Lady, Mrs. Ulysses S. Grant, stated, "I love the dear old

The second floor oval room has always been a favorite room of White House families. President Rutherford B. Hayes and his family listen to Secretary of Interior Carl Schurz play the piano in this 1880 print.

BETTY C. MONKMAN

house and, if I could have my way, would never have it changed." But shortly after she moved into the house in 1869 she began to make it a home. "I at last had the furniture arranged in suites," she wrote, "so that each room would have its own set. I found it widely scattered in the upper chambers."[23] President Dwight Eisenhower recalled that his family "liked the place and all it stood for . . . it conveyed to us much of the dignity, the simple greatness of America."[24]

One of the rooms families used on a daily basis was the second-floor oval room, with its beautiful views south toward the Potomac River. It was here that John and Abigail Adams held their first White House receptions. It was a ladies' parlor in Jackson's time, a place where Emily Donelson, his White House hostess, received callers. Mrs. Millard Fillmore was the first to make it a family library, and Mrs. Grant called it her "usual sitting room," where "General Grant would bring a caller who was interesting or important or who had inquired of me."[25] The Rutherford B. Hayes family made it a room for family gatherings every evening and had hymn sings there on Sunday.

Personal photographs and objects made it home to many families. It was Mrs. Theodore Roosevelt's favorite room, and the Tafts used it a great deal, especially when there were guests. Mrs. Taft installed Oriental tapestries and furniture they had brought from the Far East to make it a personal and livable space. "Many Presidents' wives have struggled in vain to make it look homelike," wrote the wife of a Washington correspondent of the White House, but "the oval-shaped sitting room on the second floor has cheerful comfort as the sun streams through its circular windows. Here are warm-toned rugs, books, sofas, chairs. It is like a comfortable living room," she observed during the Harding era.[26]

For a brief time in the 1880s, the second-floor oval room served as the president's study, a use this room would not be put to again until Franklin Roosevelt filled it with his favorite collections of marine paintings, ship models, and gifts from heads of state. It was a room in which many

President William Howard Taft's family made the second floor oval room their home by filling it with personal objects reflecting the Tafts' own interests and taste.

momentous meetings were conducted, important decisions made, and personal guests entertained. President Truman continued to use it as an office but included a piano, a favorite form of relaxation. In 1961, after its use as an office in the 1930s and 1940s, it was furnished as a formal drawing room with late eighteenth- and early nineteenth-century French objects,

BETTY C. MONKMAN

President Franklin D. Roosevelt converted the second floor oval room to an office, which he filled with marine paintings, ship models, and gifts from heads of state.

reflecting Mrs. John F. Kennedy's tastes and interests. It became a room in which distinguished guests were entertained and special family events held. It continues to be used for such purposes to the present day.

THE PUBLIC ROOMS

The state rooms—those areas used for public entertaining and ceremony— have reflected the changing tastes of Americans as well as the personal tastes of White House residents. In the nineteenth century the most fashionable designs of the day were often incorporated into the rooms with funds allocated by Congress for such purposes. When a style became outdated and no longer in fashion, the furnishings were replaced with new objects and often discarded at sales. The choice of objects was restricted only by the funds available and, after 1826, by an act of Congress that stipulated that all objects be of domestic manufacture as far as possible.

Perhaps the philosophy of furnishing the home of the president was best expressed by William Lee, who assisted James Monroe in acquiring objects for the building in 1818. He wrote to Congress: "In furnishing a government house, care should be taken to purchase substantial heavy furniture, which

Large presidential receptions, such as this 1857 event, were held in the East Room when Congress was in session.

BETTY C. MONKMAN

should always remain in its place and form as it were part of the house, such as could be handed down through a succession of Presidents, suited to the dignity and character of the nation."[27]

Certainly, the objects James Monroe purchased in France met these criteria. Many of the furnishings made by noted craftsmen of Napoleonic France have remained among the most treasured items in the President's House. The gilded bronze ornaments and porcelain vases grace the public rooms, and the gilded furniture sets the style of the Blue Room. After the rebuilding of the White House following its destruction by the British in 1814, President Monroe sought to create a setting for a strong and stable presidency and nation.

Charles Bulfinch, the architect of the Capitol, commented on the refurbished house in 1818: "I found it spacious and noble, well arranged both for parade and family convenience; the finishing and furnishings rich but not heavy."[28] A more glowing account was reported by a visitor who had attended a drawing room at the same time: "I vow I felt as if I were in a fairy palace; such splendor, such brilliancy, such magnificence—oh! it is beyond description."[29] In the late 1860s a Washington guidebook pronounced, "Nearly all parts of the house are accessible to visitors, and something of interest may be found in all apartments."[30]

The East Room has always been the most public of the state floor rooms. In the nineteenth century it was often the only room open for viewing by the public. Designed by the architect James Hoban to be the Public Audience Room, it has seen the presentation of diplomatic envoys such as the Japanese in 1860, troops quartered for a time during the Civil War, delegations of Indians received by the president, promenades at nineteenth-century receptions, and receiving lines in every administration. It stood bare and uninhabitable before the fire of 1814. When the house was reconstructed in 1817–18, Hoban had the walls plastered and designed a plaster frieze of anthemia, which appears in all nineteenth-century views of the room. The room was used but not furnished. According to an 1825 inventory, the room was full of cobwebs, benches, a clothes press, and pine tables. Not until Andrew Jackson was president would Congress appropriate funds to furnish the room. A British visitor at a presidential levee remarked on the unfinished and bare interior: "Even the walls were left in their unpainted plaster. Here was a degree of republican simplicity beyond what I should have expected, as it seemed out of character with what I saw elsewhere."[31]

In 1829, the first year of Jackson's term, a Philadelphia firm, Louis Veron, supplied furnishings, lemon-colored wallpaper, blue-and-yellow draperies with gilded eagle cornices, four new marble mantels, overmantel mirrors, and the highlight of the room, three chandeliers whose style was characterized as entirely new. They were fitted for gas in 1849 and remained in the room until 1873. The room was reported as "lately fitted up in a very neat manner" in 1830 and as being "splendidly furnished" in 1839. "Here congregates," an observer noted, "all the fashion that flocks to Washington during the sessions of Congress."[32] A congressman who attended a levee in 1861 recounted his visit:

> Here you meet the great men of the nation—*and some great women*—together with the most humble—as these receptions are open to all. . . . the center of this large room is used on such occasions as a grand promenade—ladies and gentlemen march to the strains of enticing music played by a most splendid band which is supported by government—Those who do not care to join in the promenade, stand, look on, and comment on the good or ill looks of this one, or that one. . . . Such is human life as seen on these occasions.[33]

The ceiling was frescoed under the direction of Thomas U. Walter in 1853, and while carpeting and draperies changed, the room retained the Jackson furnishings until the Grant administration, when in preparation for the wedding of Nellie Grant the room received a very different appearance, referred to in a 1874 Washington guidebook as "pure Greek." The ceiling

BETTY C. MONKMAN

The East Room redecorated by Louis Comfort Tiffany in the summer months of 1882, under the direction of President Arthur, the sophisticated New Yorker whose real interest was in improving the appearance of the house. Arthur had an appetite for the high Aesthetic style of interior decoration current in urban centers of style at the time—the sensitivity to color and the historical and exotic themes. The bold, and even whimsical, decorator Tiffany, in the selection of traditional motifs for the East Room, chose a floral Brussels carpet in intricate Oriental patterns, while the ceiling was painted in what was to resemble Pompeian mosaics in a classical theme. These antique colors and patterns were praised as being in keeping with the room's "old colonial" character, and President Arthur's interest in the house continued as long as he occupied it.

FURNITURE AND INTERIORS

was divided into three sections by large beams and fluted Corinthian columns, and new glass chandeliers were added. In 1882 Louis C. Tiffany painted the ceiling in silver and various tones of ivory and covered the walls with gray painted paper highlighted in gold.

By the 1890s the East Room in full Victorian splendor was the only state room open to the public. As the century turned, decisions were made in the Theodore Roosevelt administration to strip the house of its late nineteenth-century interiors. McKim, Mead & White, the architectural firm responsible for the work, created what was termed a colonial revival interior, but the East Room was an interior copied from an eighteenth-century French chateau. They installed enameled wood paneling and an ornamental stucco ceiling as well as new mantels, chandeliers, and an oak floor. It was a clear contrast to the previous room, and although Charles McKim claimed that the changes were based on historical precedents in the house, the 1902 interior bore no resemblance to the Monroe-Jackson room of the early nineteenth century.

The character of this new East Room would, however, be retained throughout the twentieth century except for modifications to the architectural elements in the room during the Truman renovation, when the paneling and ceiling ornamentation were simplified, new mantels were installed, and the chandeliers shortened. The Commission on the Renovation of the Executive Mansion stated that it wanted the room to "present a more restrained appearance."[34] The only changes since 1952 have been in drapery designs and fabrics and the faux-marbling of the mantels.

In contrast to the public East Room, the Red Room was a family parlor in the nineteenth century, a place for the First Lady to receive callers and for the family to gather to visit friends or listen to musical performances by artists visiting the city. An 1897 visitor noted that the room had a "pleasant, occupied air not possessed by the more public Blue and Green Rooms."[35] This was true earlier in the century as well. The first use of the room was

BETTY C. MONKMAN

128

as the president's antechamber—a waiting room for appointments to presidents Adams and Jefferson.

By the Madison administration it had assumed its character as a parlor; a guest in 1813 noted the "elegant and delicate furniture" upholstered in bright yellow satin and curtains of sunflower yellow damask.[36] The decorations of the room were the result of Benjamin Latrobe's collaboration with Dolley Madison, who used the room for her entertainments.

An 1825 inventory continued to refer to the room as the yellow drawing room but mentioned window curtains of elegant red silk and furniture upholstered in crimson cloth. By the Polk administration of the late 1840s, the room had acquired the name Red Room or Washington Parlor because the large Gilbert Stuart portrait of George Washington hung there. Visitors described the room, with its crimson velvet curtains and red plush upholstery, as "warm and comfortable."[37] In the room were several of the French gilded bronze candelabra and porcelain vases that had been there since Monroe's time.

In 1866 Andrew Johnson's daughter, Martha Patterson, undertook to refurbish the room. A White House aide commented that she wanted "no mingling of the old and new."[38] She had the walls papered with black-and-gold panels and bought a suite of revival furniture in the French taste. The earliest photographs of the room taken in the 1870s show a grand piano and a family portrait by William Cogswell that belonged to President and Mrs. Grant. In the Hayes administration a new suite of gilded furniture by the Herter Brothers firm in New York graced the room, as did a silver centerpiece that had been selected by Mrs. Grant at the Centennial Exposition in Philadelphia in 1876.

This was the setting when Chester Arthur called on Louis Comfort Tiffany to make the room presentable to his sophisticated tastes. The result was described as dark and moody, with French embossed paper of "Pompeian" red. The ceiling was decorated in tempera colors with stars in gold

The Red Room, one of the state rooms, was used as a family parlor by White House residents in the nineteenth century. A portrait of the Grant family and their piano appear in this photograph of the early 1870s.

and a suggestion of stripes in the border. The highlight of the room was the cherry mantel, stained dark red and inlaid with tiles in tones of brown, amber, and reddish brown. Above the mantel was a mosaic of glass that gave the appearance of being studded with gems. Eleven years later, Mrs. Grover Cleveland changed the wall colors to brighter red, and in 1891 the old gasolier was replaced with a lighting fixture wired for electricity.

BETTY C. MONKMAN

By the end of the nineteenth century, the architect Glenn Brown noted, the decoration was totally out of sympathy with the house and reminded one of a Pullman Palace car.[39] Brown would support the 1902 changes in this and other rooms. New cornices and white enameled wainscotting replaced the array of pattern of the late nineteenth century. Throughout the early twentieth century, different shades of red were installed in the room, and reproduction furniture of various styles continued in use until 1961, when the Fine Arts Committee formed by Mrs. John F. Kennedy recommended that the room be furnished as an American parlor of the period 1815–35. Except for a slight change of color and new draperies in 1970, the room retains this style today. Although for most purposes families no longer use the room as they did in the nineteenth century, it still functions as a parlor and arena for state affairs.

White House interiors have never been static period rooms. They have evolved and changed to reflect changes in the country and the tastes of the presidents and their families who have lived and worked in the President's House and who have met the ceremonial obligations of the presidency, much as the founders of the nation envisioned two hundred years ago. In these rooms the president of the United States receives foreign heads of state and ambassadors, signs treaties, greets a wide variety of guests, communicates to the American people, and conducts the business of the country as presidents have done since John Adams first occupied the house in 1800.

NOTES

1. *Statutes at Large,* vol. I (1790), 139.

2. Washington to David Stuart, March 8, 1792, in John C. Fitzpatrick, ed., *Writings of Washington, 1745–1799* (Washington: Government Printing Office, 1939), 31:505.

3. Commissioners of the District of Columbia to municipal authorities in Bordeaux, France, January 4, 1793, in Lois Craig, *The Federal Presence: Architecture, Politics, and Symbols in United States Government Buildings* (Cambridge: MIT Press, 1978), 32.

4. Gouverneur Morris to George Washington, January 24, 1790, in Susan Detweiler, *George Washington's Chinaware* (New York: Abrams), 112.

5. *Morrison's Stranger's Guide to the City of Washington and Its Vicinity* (Washington: W. M. Morrison, 1855), 39.

6. Oliver Wolcott to Mrs. Wolcott, July 4, 1800, in Sally S. Mackall, *Early Days of Washington* (Washington: Neale, 1899), 284.

7. Casimir Bohn, *Bohn's Hand-Book of Washington* (Washington: Casimir Bohn, 1856), 33.

8. Jonathan Elliot, *Historical Sketches of the Ten Miles Square Forming the District of Columbia* (Washington: J. Elliott, Jr., 1830), 163–64.

9. Charles William Janson, *The Stranger in America* (London: James Cundee, Albion, 1807), 206.

10. Caleb Atwater, *The Indians of the Northwest* (Columbus, Ohio, 1850), 122; cited in Herman J. Viola, *Diplomats in Buckskins: A History of Indian Delegations in Washington City* (Washington: Smithsonian Institution Press, 1981), 95.

11. Samuel Lorenzo Knapp [Ignatius Loyola Robertson], *Sketches of Public Characters Drawn from the Living and the Dead* (New York: E. Bliss, 1830), 111–12.

12. Jean H. Baker, *Mary Todd Lincoln, A Biography* (New York: Norton, 1987), 182.

13. Margaret Leech, *Reveille in Washington, 1860–1865* (New York: Book-of-the-Month Club, 1989), 8.

14. Nathalie Sedgwick Colby, *Remembering* (Boston: Little, Brown, 1938), 199.

15. Louis Arthur Coolidge and James Burton Reynolds, *The Show at Washington* (Washington: Washington Publishing Co., 1894), 6.

16. Max Berger, *The British Traveller in America, 1836–1860* (Gloucester, Mass.: Peter Smith, 1964), 89.

17. James Stuart, *Three Years in North America* (Edinburgh: Robert Cadell, 1833), 2:77.

18. *Philp's Washington Described,* ed. William D. Haley (New York: Rudd & Carleton, 1861), 199.

19. Stuart, *Three Years,* 77.

20. Jonathan Elliot, *Historical Sketches,* 163.

21. Although White House inventories were taken as early as 1801, Mrs. Herbert Hoover was the first resident of the White House to attempt to compile a record of the history of objects in the President's House. When Mrs. John F.

Kennedy raised concerns about the loss of so much of the contents of the building, Congress passed legislation in 1961 (Public Law 87-286, 87th Congress, September 22, 1961) to preserve objects from sale or disposal. Congressional appropriations for furnishings were seldom adequate in the nineteenth century, and sales continued until 1903.

22. Mrs. William Howard Taft, *Recollections of Full Years* (New York: Dodd, Mead, 1914), 342.

23. Julia Dent Grant, *The Personal Memoirs of Julia Dent Grant (Mrs. Ulysses S. Grant)*, ed. John Y. Simon (New York: Putnam, 1975), 174.

24. Dwight D. Eisenhower, *Mandate for Change, 1953–1956* (New York: Doubleday, 1963), 259.

25. Julia Dent Grant, *Personal Memoirs*, 180.

26. Olive Ewing Clapper, *Washington Tapestry* (New York: Whittlesey House, 1946), 61.

27. James Monroe, Message to Congress, February 10, 1818. House of Representatives report 91, 15th Cong., 1st sess.

28. *The Life and Letters of Charles Bulfinch, Architect*, ed. Ellen Susan Bulfinch (Boston: Houghton, Mifflin, 1896), 215.

29. George Watterston, *The L . . . Family at Washington; or, A Winter in the Metropolis* (Washington: Davis and Force, 1822), 81.

30. *Guide to Washington City and Vicinity* (Washington: John F. Ellis, 1868), 40.

31. Captain Basil Hall, *Travels in North America in the Years 1827 and 1828* (Edinburgh: Cadell, 1829), 14.

32. Jonathan Elliot, *Historical Sketches*, 161, and *Public Buildings and Statuary of the Government: The Public Buildings and Architectural Ornaments of the Capitol of the United States at the City of Washington* (Washington: F. Hass, 1839), 37.

33. James E. English to Caroline English, July 18, 1861. Typewritten copy in Office of the Curator, the White House.

34. *Report of the Commission on the Renovation of the Executive Mansion* (Washington: Government Printing Office, 1952), 60.

35. C. O'Conor-Eccles, "President and Mrs. McKinley at the White House," *Woman at Home* (October 1897), 5.

36. *The Diary of Elbridge Gerry, Jr.*, ed. Claude B. Bowers (New York: Brentano's, 1927), 180.

37. Diary of Elizabeth Dixon (Mrs. James Dixon), December 6, 1845, type-

written manuscript, Connecticut Historical Society, Hartford, Conn. Copy in Office of the Curator, the White House.

38. Benjamin Brown French to Thaddeus Stevens, January 5, 1867. Letters Sent, vol. 16, Records of the Office of Public Buildings, record group 42, National Archives.

39. Glenn Brown, "The New White House," *Harper's Weekly* (July 14, 1906), 990.

SIX

Furnishing the Executive Mansion: Nineteenth-Century Washington Sources

WILLIAM G. ALLMAN

INTEGRAL to the functioning of the White House as residence and office, stage and landmark, is the appearance, the furnishing, of its interior spaces. Although given a more historical character in the twentieth century, the White House in the nineteenth century was a contemporary home through and through. As such, it was refurbished not just in response to unavoidable wear and tear but also to changes of style and the tastes of the First Families.

What part did the local business community play in this nineteenth-century decorative history? As the seat of government with no industrial base, Washington in no way rivaled Philadelphia, New York, or Baltimore as a center of wealth and commerce. So as the First Families, temporary occupants at that, sought to leave their mark on the White House interiors, they often entrusted refurbishings to designers and suppliers from those established centers of fashion.

Not surprisingly, decorative services—upholstering, window draping, fitting carpets, gilding—were often provided by local concerns, even when the furnishings and textiles themselves might be secured elsewhere. But there were times when fine durable goods were acquired from local craftsmen or merchants. Even though shopping locally was usually considered a sign of economizing, the business community in the District of Columbia did have an important, if less well known, role in the decorative history of the White House, some of the highlights of which may help to flesh out that story.

1800–1814

When President and Mrs. John Adams moved into the unfinished President's House in November 1800, the official furnishings—American, French, and English, brought from Philadelphia—were not adequate for the rooms available during their four-month stay. Even then, as would be the case throughout the century, congressman held differing opinions on the subject of appropriations for presidential furnishings. On March 1, 1801, the House of Representatives met to consider the funding of further acquisitions, some calling for a supplement to the six thousand dollars remaining from a fifteen-thousand-dollar appropriation, others saying that no more was needed. Among the latter, Nathaniel Macon of North Carolina was reported to have remarked that surely a proposal for a larger presidential salary would soon follow to "bring him up to the style of his furniture."[1]

All positions on funding, however, included a reliance on "the proceeds of such furniture, as being unfit for use, might be sold."[2] Regularly authorized by Congress, sales of "such part of the furniture . . . belonging to [the president's] household as may be decayed, out of repair"[3] provided business for a number of Washington auctioneers until 1903, a practice by which many White House objects passed into private hands. Although the most common consumers at the earlier sales were local merchants and the keepers of hotels, boardinghouses, and taverns, later in the century they would be joined by crowds of people actually seeking souvenirs from a White House with, by then, an acknowledged historical importance.

President Thomas Jefferson did much in the following eight years to

WILLIAM G. ALLMAN

improve the interiors, but there is little record of the sources of the goods and materials used, although much certainly came from Philadelphia. One exception was the 1808 purchase of unidentified "silverware" for $113 from the most prominent local silversmith, Charles A. Burnett,[4] who had moved about 1800 from Alexandria, in the Virginia portion of the District of Columbia, to Georgetown on the Maryland side, presumably to be closer to potential government clients. He would remain an important White House vendor until at least 1833.

To assist in creating an impressive three-room first-floor suite for entertaining, President and Mrs. James Madison called on the architect Benjamin Henry Latrobe, the superintendent of public buildings, who shopped during the spring of 1809 in Baltimore and Philadelphia but wrote of difficulties in finding suitable drapery fabrics even in those largest commercial centers.[5] For the principal oval drawing room (now the Blue Room), there eventually came mirrors from New York, draperies from Philadelphia, and painted furniture made to his own designs by the Findlay shop in Baltimore.

Even at this early date, however, local business people may have expected that coveted White House patronage should be bestowed on them. That the oval room draperies were not made locally may have contributed to an embarrassing situation for Latrobe created by Mrs. Sweeney, "the proprietress of the most elegant upholstery shop in Washington."[6] Mrs. Madison, in reply to a letter from Latrobe, wrote of Mrs. Sweeney's malicious gossip: "I can account for Mrs. Sweeny's mis-information to you [that Mrs. Madison was upset with his absences in Philadelphia], only by supposing her offended at my leaving her but little to do, in the house."[7]

1814–1825

On August 24, 1814, during the War of 1812, the British burned the White House and the public property therein, with the exception of the Gilbert Stuart portrait of George Washington (now in the East Room) and the oval room draperies, both saved at Mrs. Madison's direction. To furnish the temporary quarters they occupied from 1815 to 1817, the Madisons relied on local sources for available furniture, mostly secondhand if one believes William Lee, the purchasing agent for President Monroe in 1817: "President Madison . . . having purchased after the government house was burnt, with the small sum allowed, only some second hand furniture whenever he could get it merely for the moment."[8]

But used furnishings in Washington were not necessarily outmoded discards or estate pieces. Often when members of the diplomatic corps departed, they sold personal property they had brought with them, events that were much enjoyed by local society. In 1815 the Madisons acquired from Louis Serurier, the French minister, a dozen chairs and a sofa for $250. Perhaps they were familiar with this seat furniture, for Serurier had occupied two of the area's most fashionable houses, Kalorama and the Octagon. In fact, he had a hand in securing the latter as the Madisons' first temporary residence, in 1814–15.[9]

For their second temporary residence, in the Seven Buildings on Pennsylvania Avenue, in 1815–17, the Madisons acquired a great deal of furniture from a Georgetown cabinetmaker, William Worthington, Jr., possibly secondhand but as likely good locally made furniture, including two settees ($90), one secretary desk ($40), one large dining table ($25), and one "large family bedstead" ($22). They also again patronized the merchant and silversmith Charles Burnett, buying fireplace equipment, glassware, and plated flatware, the cost of which was partially defrayed by the common practice of trading in silverware, usually damaged pieces, for their metal content alone, in this case sixty-eight ounces.[10]

In 1817 President and Mrs. James Monroe, in preparing to move into the rebuilt White House, may have faced an even greater need than had the Adamses in 1800 to provide, not just augment, the available government furnishings. Their purchasing agent, William Lee, in justifying the extensive new acquisitions, did not speak well of any of the local purchases made by the Madisons: "In the furniture of the houses occupied by President Madi-

1. On the east side of the White House sits the picturesque Jacqueline Kennedy Garden, often used as an informal reception area by First Ladies. The garden's rectangular lawn is surrounded by trees and shrubs, and by flowers that are changed with the seasons. Additionally, a holly osmanthus hedge and a row of lindens provide shade for the colonnade connecting the East Wing with the mansion.

2. The West Terrace has often been a sumptuous backdrop for outdoor dinners. The Tafts were the first to hold dinners on the rooftop terrace, but many first families have entertained outdoors. The glittery scene shown here is that of a barbecue given by President and Mrs. Jimmy Carter during a visit by the Japanese prime minister in 1979.

3. The Red Room, one of four state reception rooms in the White House, contains several pieces of furniture from the New York workshop of cabinetmaker Charles-Honoré Lannuier, the most notable being the rare circular table with an inlaid marble top. An 1842 portrait by Henry Inman of Angelica Singleton Van Buren, President Martin Van Buren's daughter-in-law and official hostess, hangs above the mantel. A white marble bust of Van Buren appears in the portrait. Hiram Powers executed three busts of Van Buren, one of which is displayed on the wall between the two windows.

4. Theodore Roosevelt's "Gentlemen's Ante-room" was remodeled in 1935 as a library, and in 1961 a committee was appointed to select works representative of a full spectrum of American thought and tradition for the use of the president, his family, and the staff. The collection is still being augmented with presidential papers. A Gilbert Stuart portrait of George Washington, painted about 1805 and donated to the White House in 1949, hangs above the fireplace.

5. The yellow and white Center Hall serves as an informal sitting room for the First Family and presidential guests, including many foreign dignitaries who are received in the Yellow Oval Room. The English octagonal pedestal writing desk, which divides the hall into two receiving rooms, dates from the eighteenth century and is made in two halves that may be separated for use against a wall. A ramp leads to the principal guest bedrooms, located above the elevated ceiling of the East Room.

6. The Oval Blue Room was completely renovated in 1995 with many furnishings in the French Empire style, the decor chosen for the room by President James Monroe in 1817. A settee and seven of the original gilded chairs fashioned for Monroe by the Parisian cabinetmaker Pierre-Antione Bellangé form the nucleus of the present furnishings.

7. Since 1902 the cabinet has met in the West Wing. This room, which looks out on the Rose Garden, has been used for the purpose since 1934. The chairs, copies of a late eighteenth-century American style, bear brass plaques with cabinet members' titles. Armand Dumaresque's painting *The Signing of the Declaration of Independence* hangs over the fireplace and is flanked by marble busts of George Washington and Benjamin Franklin.

8. The East Room, largest and most formal of the state reception rooms, normally contains little furniture and traditionally is used for large gatherings. The Steinway grand piano with gilt American eagle supports was designed by Eric Gugler at the suggestion of Franklin D. Roosevelt and given to the White House in 1938 by the manufacturer. The portrait of George Washington is one of several replicas made by Gilbert Stuart of his "Lansdowne" portrait. Also visible is John Singer Sargent's 1903 portrait of Theodore Roosevelt.

9. The Lincoln Bedroom, actually used by Lincoln as an office and Cabinet Room, is decorated primarily with American Victorian furnishings from the years 1850–70. President Truman converted the space into a bedroom. The imposing rosewood bed is more than eight feet long and almost six feet wide. It is part of a large quantity of furniture purchased by Mrs. Lincoln in 1861. The bed and matching marble-topped table are adorned with carved birds, grapevines, and flowers.

10. Presidential portraits, a cut-glass chandelier, and red carpet on marble steps decorate the main stairway. This elegant passage between the family and state floors is often used on ceremonial occasions: the president greets his guests of honor in the Yellow Oval Room before they descend the stairs to pose for photographers or to meet other guests.

11. The Cross Hall, separated from the North Entrance Hall by a colonnade, runs from the State Dining Room to the East Room. The Adam-style cut-glass chandeliers were made in London about 1790. An Italian settee similar to furniture once owned by President Monroe stands beneath J. Anthony Wills's 1967 portrait of Dwight D. Eisenhower.

12. The Oval Office reflects each change of administration more dramatically than any other area of the White House, except possibly the private quarters. Most presidents fill the office with personal mementos and a desk of their own choosing. A specially woven oval rug bears the presidential seal. A "porthole" portrait of George Washington by Rembrandt Peale hangs above the mantel.

13. The Green Room, a first-floor parlor now most often used for small teas and receptions, was completely refurbished in 1971. The inventory of February 1801 indicates it was first used as a "Lodging Room." Thomas Jefferson used it as a dining room with a "canvass floor cloth, painted Green," foreshadowing the present color scheme. It has also been a sitting room and a card room. The furniture, in the styles of the Federal period, includes many pieces attributed to the famous New York cabinetmaker Duncan Phyfe.

14. The Diplomatic Reception Room, one of three oval rooms in the Residence, serves as an entrance to the White House from the south grounds for the family and for ambassadors arriving to present their credentials to the president. The panoramic wallpaper, "Views of North America," was first printed in 1834 by Jean Zuber et Cie. in Rixheim, Alsace, and includes landscapes of the Natural Bridge of Virginia, Niagara Falls, New York Bay, West Point, and Boston Harbor.

Bergère or armchair, gilded beechwood, made by Pierre-Antoine Bellangé, Paris; purchased by President Monroe in 1817 for the oval drawing room, now the Blue Room. The set was sold at auction in Washington in 1860; seven pieces have been returned to the White House since 1961.

Armchair, mahogany, made by William King, Jr., of Georgetown. One from a suite of twenty-four chairs and four sofas purchased in 1818 from the local cabinet-maker for the East Room. They were disposed of during Grant's redecoration in 1873; three chairs from the set have been returned to the White House since 1961.

son there was no resource. . . . The chairs, tables, bedsteads, &c. had been so long in use as to be fit only for servants' rooms." He wrote of being able to reuse but a few dining chairs, a "set of old French chairs" (probably those from Serurier), two mirrors, two pier tables, and a sideboard.[11] One must wonder whether the Madison property, such as Worthington's 1815

FURNISHING THE EXECUTIVE MANSION

furniture, was truly worn out or merely not suitable in the eyes of the Monroes.

Partial to the French style, having served twice in Paris, the Monroes ordered a large quantity of French furnishings, including a giltwood suite by Pierre-Antoine Bellangé of Paris for the Oval Room. With nearly the entire twenty-thousand-dollar appropriation consumed, Lee defended these French purchases:

> in furnishing a government house, care should be taken to purchase
> substantial heavy furniture, which should always remain in its place
> and form as it were part of the house, such as could be handed
> down through a succession of Presidents, suited to the dignity and
> character of the nation. In the end this sort of furniture is the most
> economical.

Curiously, he gave the objects a shorter lifetime than they would actually enjoy: "so substantial that some of them will last and be handsome for 20 years or more." Most of the Bellangé suite would not be sold at auction until more than forty years later, in 1860 (since 1961 seven pieces have been retrieved for the Blue Room). More of the other French objects—tableware, clocks, candelabra—survived the auctions, remaining continuously in the White House collection.[12]

At least one partisan newspaper defended these purchases, although omitting, probably intentionally, any mention of the prominent Bellangé suite:

> Several of the articles which constitute the furniture of the Presi-
> dent's House have been imported from France, but they consist only
> of such articles as cannot, in the present state of our manufactures,
> be made in this country—such as looking glasses; silks and damasks
> for curtains and chairs; some ornamental clocks, and a piano.

WILLIAM G. ALLMAN

The same newspaper then credited the new furniture for the rest of the house to local craftsmen at reasonable costs:

> All the furniture of the small saloon, sitting room, dining room, and bed rooms, are made, or making, in the city of Washington. There is not a chair in the President's house which has cost more than such as are to be seen in the drawing rooms of many of our merchants in Philadelphia and New York.[13]

Among the local suppliers was the cabinetmaker William King, Jr., of Georgetown. In keeping with Lee's aspirations for appropriate institutional furniture, King produced in 1818 a suite of heavy mahogany seat furniture—twenty-four armchairs and four sofas—for the East Room for $1,584. The King furniture cost 40 percent less than the gilded and somewhat more ornamented Bellangé furniture—armchairs at $33 (Bellangé at $54), sofas at $198 ($337).[14]

Unfortunately, as funds ran low the decoration of the East Room was abandoned; as a result, the King furniture waited eleven years, until 1829, for its finish upholstery. Chairs from this suite can be seen in some of the earliest interior photos, taken in the East Room in the late 1860s, before their disposal in the Grant redecoration of that room in 1873. Fortunately, three chairs have been retrieved for the White House collection, one having descended from the Grants' decorator, another in the family of John T. Ford, who had acquired parts of the suite for his theaters in Washington and Baltimore.

William Worthington, Jr., was again an important supplier, providing bookcases ($200) and a large dining table and sixteen chairs ($285). But his work was not without problems, as he faced some dispute over the $425 charge for a sideboard, a bed, and five sets of dressing tables and washstands. He called on the Washington cabinetmaker Benjamin M. Belt (his apprentice in 1802 and now a White House supplier as well), who examined

The East Room, ca. 1869, soon after the Civil War, with the draperies down and the William King chairs slipcovered for the summer months. These seasonal changes were provided by Washington merchants such as Charles Alexander.

his pieces at the White House and endorsed the bill, claiming the prices to be "Customary in the City of Washington"; payment resulted.[15]

A new fifteen-piece suite of seat furniture for the sitting room (now Red Room) was upholstered by a young French immigrant, Charles Alexander, who received unusual financial assistance from Lee: "To aid him in his work

WILLIAM G. ALLMAN

I endorsed a note for him of $200, as he is wanting of money being a new beginner." Although his bill was submitted in French with his name spelled "Alexandre," he Americanized it to "Alexander" when signing for payment. Thus began a long career in Washington that frequently included making the seasonal decorative changes at the White House. As was common to all great houses in preparation for the summer, seat furniture was slipcovered and draperies were taken down, carpets taken up, and lighting fixtures and mirrors sometimes bagged or draped against the ravages of summer dust and flies. Then in the fall the process was reversed.[16]

Alexander's long service to the White House would produce, however, some controversy in 1851 during the Fillmore administration. William Easby, on becoming the commissioner of public buildings and asking who usually did work for the White House, was told the ubiquitous Alexander. He hired him, unaware that another local upholsterer, David Baird, had been doing White House work. He had to write to Baird to explain the situation and assure him that he had not been dismissed.[17]

William Lee explained the Monroes' sizable investment of more than three thousand dollars in silver and gilded silver:

> In the house of a private gentleman plate is an expensive thing, be-
> cause the interest on the capital placed on it would pay for all the
> breakage of china and earthen ware. But in a house like that of the
> President of the United States, where you are obliged to entertain
> daily and keep a large number of servants, plate is an article of econ-
> omy and pays for itself in the course of a few years. . . .[18]

About one-third of the funds went to Charles Burnett, principally for six quite considerable dishes (356 ounces total) costing $712. Although these have not survived in the White House collection, three of six Burnett salt spoons remain as the oldest pieces of American silver continuously used in the White House. Again, much of the cost was defrayed by supplying 671 ounces of silver ($770).[19]

In securing a supplemental appropriation of thirty thousand dollars, President Monroe reported to the Congress: "The furniture, in its kind and extent, is thought to be an object, not less deserving attention than the building for which it is intended. . . . the sum already appropriated, has proved altogether inadequate."[20] All in all, expenditures made in Washington from 1817 to 1820, including nine thousand dollars spent on some of the Monroes' personal furnishings, represented about half the total. An additional one-sixth was spent domestically—in Pittsburgh (glassware) and Philadelphia (linens, carpeting, glassware, flatware, draperies). But the remaining one-third was spent in France, a much-touted fact that largely prompted an 1826 Act of Congress stating: "All furniture purchased for the use of the President's House must be, as far as practicable, of American or Domestic manufacture."[21]

But even with controversy over costs and foreign sources, the newly appointed senator John Taylor of Virginia did not find the White House interiors sumptuous only a few years later, in 1823:

> My curiosity induced me to take the liberty of asking to be shewn the furniture, about which so much was said. That affair was quite exaggerated. The quantity is barely sufficient to save the country from the disgrace of building a great palace with a naked interior. . . . The quality of most of it very much resembles that of a private gentleman's furniture.[22]

Silver salt spoon made by Charles A. Burnett, Georgetown; believed to be from a group of six acquired in 1817 by James Monroe for the newly rebuilt White House.

WILLIAM G. ALLMAN

That Washington could meet most decorating needs, if not necessarily all whims or fancies, was demonstrated in 1826 when John Quincy Adams, Jr., wrote on an accounting of expenditures in the first year of his father's administration: "the expenditures have all been made with an eye to the strictest economy. Scarcely an Article has been purchased which was not indispensably necessary; everything has been secured, when possible, in this City or District, in order to avoid the expenses of transportation." On that listing, lamps, fire grates, and a parlor suite by Michael Bouvier from Philadelphia and a secretary-bookcase by John Needles of Baltimore were supplemented by pieces from many of the prominent local craftsmen including silver from Burnett and furniture from Worthington, Belt, and Henry V. Hill.[23] A newspaper advertisement which Hill ran that year cited that he had "for the last twelve years received a liberal share of the public patronage." It apparently helped little, for he lost his home to a debtor's sale only three months later.[24]

For President Andrew Jackson, the prominent Philadelphia firm Louis Veron & Co. was entrusted with nearly all the decorative work, costing about $30,000. In 1829 the firm finally finished the East Room ($9,300), which included the upholstering of the 1818 William King seat furniture and the provision of seven tables by Anthony Quervelle (four extant). In 1833, when Veron papered the public rooms and provided new American glassware and French china ($16,600), one local vendor, Darius Clagett & Co., did snare $3,000 worth of business in Brussels carpeting and borders, drapery and upholstery fabrics. At the same time, James Green, who operated cabinet shops both in Alexandria and in Washington, provided $575 worth of rather prominent furniture: one sofa and twelve chairs for the "Audience Room" and forty dining chairs.[25] Green had advertised his work in 1829, not claiming to rival furniture from the bigger cities, but citing its inspiration and local merit: "Fashionable Cabinet Furniture . . . unrivalled by any manufactured in this District, being made after the most modern style of northern work by superior workmen, of select and beautiful materials."[26]

In December of that year a great quantity of old silver was sold, not in Washington, as was usual, but in Philadelphia through George W. South. Perhaps a bigger market was deemed necessary for such a volume: 350 pieces of flatware, 59 of hollowware, totaling 4,662 ounces, which realized $3,666. At the same time, however, furniture and glassware were sold in Washington through P. Mauro & Son, who charged the White House an $11 "proportion of expenses," explaining that "to display the Goods to the best advantage, I rented a room on the [Pennsylvania] Avenue, had tables made and [bought] baize to cover them. . . ."[27] In turn, these "proceeds of decayed property" financed an important $4,000 purchase from the diplomatic community: a magnificent collection of French Empire silver by Martin-Guillaume Biennais, obtained from the estate of the Russian minister, the Baron de Tuyll, much of which remains in the White House collection today.[28]

The considerable patronage of President Martin Van Buren went largely to suppliers in New York City, expenditures that helped make the subject of White House furnishings a political issue in the 1840 election year. In an April 4 speech in the House of Representatives on the "Regal Splendor of the President's Palace," a Whig congressman, Charles Ogle of Pennsylvania, spoke extensively about acquisitions for the President's House since 1817 in order to attack the life-style of President Van Buren.[29]

One prominent subject was the gilt flatware from the de Tuyll service, acquired not by Van Buren but by Jackson. "*They may be pure gold*, though I am inclined to believe otherwise" (Ogle's emphasis). In response to congressional pressure, William Noland, the commissioner of public buildings, called on the local business community in the person of "Mr. [Robert] Keyworth [an occasional supplier to the White House from 1837 to 1850], a respectable gold and silver smith of the City," to certify that the dessert flatware was not gold, but silver gilt.[30]

WILLIAM G. ALLMAN

Late in many administrations, purchases were made locally to offset losses or sales, thereby providing a more habitable and functional house for the next occupants. For example, the local cabinetmaker Edwin Green provided two "French Maple Bedsteads" ($22) in the last week of President Van Buren's term, and another such bed ($16) during President William Henry Harrison's one-month term. Green operated the "old Cabinet Manufactory" (formerly operated by James Green, who had supplied furniture to the Jackson White House), where he stocked or would "manufacture to order" a large line of objects, including "French [Maple and common] high and low post Bedsteads," "of the best workmanship and materials, which

Silver waste bowl made by Robert Keyworth, Washington, ca. 1837–51. The acquisition of this bowl, sugar tongs, and matching creamer, probably from a full tea service, is not documented.

he will sell (especially for cash) as low as at any manufactory in the Union."[31]

But government payment was never speedy, which in 1841 caused some confusion when three presidents held office within the space of a month. Although the bill from the Alexandria merchant Hugh Smith & Co. was issued during the last week of Van Buren's term, not until June did President John Tyler personally authorize payment, misattributing the several dozens of "best cut" glasses and eight sets of "Best Toilet Ware" to the "articles purchased for the President's House during the lifetime of the late President [Harrison]."[32]

Naturally, White House funerals generated spur-of-the-moment business for local craftsmen and merchants. For Harrison, the first president to die in office, the funeral was staged by the merchant Alexander Hunter, who hired the upholsterer John Williams to outfit the coffin and create mourning ornaments, while Darius Clagett, who had provided carpeting under Jackson and fabrics under Van Buren, draped the chandeliers and mirrors with black crepe.[33]

When Abigail Fillmore got Congress to appropriate two thousand dollars in 1850 for the purchase of the first official White House library, the books were installed in the second floor oval room on five hundred dollars' worth of bookcases made by the Washington cabinetmaker William McLean Cripps, who had provided furniture as early as 1825.[34] Generally, however, midcentury marked the end of the era of furniture made in local shops. In the second half of the century, although custom-made furniture was provided by the nonlocal decorators, furniture acquired locally would come from retailers marketing the products of nonlocal furniture factories.

1851–1881

Although most of the furnishings acquired for the James K. Polks (1845–49) and the Franklin Pierces (1853–57) had come from New York merchants, suppliers in Philadelphia were the choice during the Buchanan administration, including G. Vollmer's "Manufactory of Fashionable Furniture" for new furniture or reupholstering in most of the principal rooms. As a result, on January 17, 1860, a local auctioneer, James C. McGuire & Co., then sold most of the 1817 Bellangé suite ($325), along with the draperies from the East, Blue, and Green Rooms ($368).[35]

After Mary Todd Lincoln visited the Washington dry-goods stores in 1861, she also realized that fine furniture was available in greater variety in New York and Philadelphia and made two shopping trips north. For the necessary decorative services, however, she relied on John Alexander (son of oft-serving Charles, who had first worked at the White House in 1817) for more than twenty-three thousand dollars' worth of work in four years, including the provision of at least three expensive suites of rosewood bedroom furniture. In fact, in 1863 both she and President Lincoln wrote endorsements for Alexander's application for work at the Capitol; Mrs. Lincoln wrote: "From the work done at the Executive Mansion by him I can certify to his competence. I ask for his application a favorable consideration." Not surprisingly, Alexander also handled the Lincoln funeral decorations.[36]

For President and Mrs. Andrew Johnson, much decorating was needed after the wear and tear of the Civil War years and the ravages of souvenir seekers who cut drapes, tore upholsteries, and pilfered china and silver while Mrs. Lincoln remained in seclusion upstairs for five weeks after her husband's assassination. Although replacement tableware was acquired through a New York retailer, E. V. Haughwout & Co., little new furniture seems to have been deemed necessary, other than three additional bedroom suites purchased from John Alexander. Decorative services, however, provided Alexander nearly $20,000 of business in 1865, and William A. Mitchell nearly $45,000 in 1866–68.[37]

In 1869 the Entrance Hall was decorated for President and Mrs. Ulysses Grant by Schutter and Rakeman, a local firm that had also worked for the Johnsons. Joseph Rakeman, an 1856 immigrant from Germany, arrived in

The Entrance Hall, ca. 1889, showing the walls and ceiling as decorated by Schutter and Rakeman in 1869. The encaustic tile floor was laid in 1880 by Hayward & Hutchinson of Washington. The stained-glass screen, installed by Louis Comfort Tiffany, was part of President Arthur's effort to redecorate the mansion in the emerging Art Nouveau style.

WILLIAM G. ALLMAN

Washington in 1857 to work with Constantino Brumidi at the Capitol. About that time he had also worked at the White House painting flowers in the East Room. He described President Buchanan as "a big old shipshead, who could use pretty rough language, especially when he saw us artists working on the scaffold. He did not like changes, and did not want to be disturbed. Fortunately he left for the summer vacation and we could then work in peace." In the 1860s Rakeman entered into partnership with Hubert Schutter in the decorating business, and in 1869 his firm patronized

Union by Constantino Brumidi, 1869, one of a pair of allegorical paintings with *Liberty*, installed in the ceiling of the White House Entrance Hall in 1869. Lightly garbed in a pure white tunic and wrapped in a cloak pale blue and red, she is the flag personified. The American bald eagle grasps arrows and an olive branch in its talons and stares fixedly up at Union—all components of the Great Seal of the United States. In the midst of yet another redecoration of the White House in 1891, during the Benjamin Harrison administration, the oils were removed, only to be discovered and reacquired in 1978.

Dinner plate from the Grant state porcelain service made by Haviland & Co., Limoges, France, ordered and supplemented through J. W. Boteler & Bro., 1870 and 1873. Boteler's mark appears on some of these pieces. Boteler also provided marked supplements to the Lincoln state china in 1873 and 1884 and supplements to the Lincoln state glassware in 1869 and 1873.

his old mentor, Brumidi, who painted two allegorical scenes for the ceiling for five hundred dollars. These paintings were removed in 1891 by the man directing a redecoration for Caroline Harrison, but were purchased back for the White House in 1978.[38]

For major acquisitions of furniture, the Grants relied on the two most

WILLIAM G. ALLMAN

prominent New York firms: Pottier & Stymus to furnish the Cabinet Room in 1869 ($6,500) and Herter Brothers for bedroom furniture in 1872 ($5,000) and a parlor suite for the Red Room in 1875 ($3,765).[39] At the local level, William Mitchell, who had done a great deal of business with the Johnson White House, provided carpets for the Red and Blue Rooms, while miscellaneous furniture came from such large retailers as W. B. Moses in 1869 and 1871 and G. W. Wight in 1873 and 1875.[40]

For seventy years, local merchants had provided everyday chinaware and some fine family ware, but none of the five specially designed state services ordered in that period. In 1870, however, the Grants chose the firm of J. W. Boteler & Bro. as the agent for ordering a formal state service from France, the first to be marked with the names of both the merchant and the manufacturer, Haviland & Co., Limoges.[41] Of the 587 pieces ordered in 1870 ($3,000), with 295 supplements in 1873, only 47 have survived in the White House today, although others are in private collections.

1881–1902

Early in the brief administration of President James Garfield, the prominent local jewelers M. W. Galt, Bro. & Co. submitted for Mrs. Garfield's consideration a teapot and the drawing of a larger version that could be made for one hundred dollars. Both the drawing and the finished product to match, made by Dominick & Haff in New York, are extant. Galt's, a firm still in operation, had evolved from a silversmithy and, as was common among such firms in the postwar years, had come to sell sterling pieces from the Northern silver factories. The first recorded sale to the White House was in 1866: two extant silver asparagus tongs made by Gorham in Providence, Rhode Island. Galt's would remain a major supplier of silver to the White House well into the twentieth century.[42]

The following month Mrs. Garfield traveled to New York to visit the fashionable Grant decorators, Pottier & Stymus and Herter Brothers. After an interview in Washington with a Herter representative, she envisioned the work she wanted done, which, after bids were submitted, went not to one of several New York firms but to the local W. B. Moses & Sons. President Garfield's assassination stalled the implementation of that contract, but President Chester Arthur was obliged to let the work go ahead in October 1881.[43]

Arthur, however, was a sophisticated New Yorker and not really satisfied. Once a bill to build a new White House failed in the Congress, he hired Louis Comfort Tiffany and his Associated Artists to redecorate or enhance most of the public rooms, $20,000 worth of work and objects from 1882 to 1884, including the famous stained-glass screen in the Entrance Hall. Nonetheless, in this same period Moses provided an additional $3,500 of furniture.[44]

Although sales of surplus property had been authorized since 1801 as a means of raising additional funds, they also served to address the problem of storage. As new furnishings arrived in the 1882 refurbishing, old property

Silver teapot made by Dominick & Haff, New York, 1881, as ordered through M. W. Galt, Bro. & Co., after Lucretia Garfield viewed a sample smaller pot and a drawing.

was sent to Duncanson Bros. auctioneers, whose advertisement of the April 14 sale mentioned, "Some of the above are very antique, and the sale is worthy of the attention of persons desiring souvenirs." The sale did draw great attention:

> Twenty-four wagon loads of old furniture and junk . . . were auction-eered yesterday. This was the first sale of Executive Mansion effects since President Buchanan's term [the 1860 sale of the Bellangé furniture]. . . . Only curiosity and a desire to examine the house-keeping of Presidents could have drawn to Ninth and D streets fully 5,000 people and caused a realization from the auction of such goods of about $3,000. . . . The bidding was as spirited on the part of prominent society people as it was by second-hand dealers and hotel keepers.[45]

Under President and Mrs. Benjamin Harrison in 1891, the W. H. Post firm of Hartford was called on to redecorate the Green Room, State Dining Room, and Entrance Hall (which included the removal of the Brumidis). The local retailer W. H. Houghton, however, provided an extant mahogany dining table for the Family Dining Room in 1890, while in 1891 M. W. Beveridge supplied a service of china made in France from a design suggested by Caroline Harrison and a service of brilliant-cut glassware made by C. Dorflinger & Sons.[46]

Although First Ladies had complained for years about the weight and incongruity of design of much of the early flatware, Mrs. Cleveland chose to act in 1894, having 141 forks, probably from the Monroe and Jackson flatware, melted down by the Treasury. These special ingots then were sent via the local retailer Harris & Shafer (formed in 1879 by two former Galt employees) to the Durgin Silver Co. in Concord, New Hampshire, which made sixteen dozen new forks in two sizes engraved with the Great Seal. Curiously, though, when additional forks were needed in 1896 and 1898, those orders went to Galt's. At that time the wife of the firm's owner was

Edith Bolling Galt, to whom the firm would pass on her husband's death in 1908; she would sell it, however, in 1915 when she married President Woodrow Wilson.[47]

Under President and Mrs. William McKinley, W. B. Moses again was actively employed, redecorating the Ushers Room in 1897 in the Flemish style with heavy oak furniture and walls and a cast metal ceiling. In 1899 it also refurbished the Blue Room in an "English colonial" decor that foreshadowed the major colonial revival renovation the house was to experience under Theodore Roosevelt in 1902. A press release described the work: "It is believed that this room has never been so harmoniously decorated."[48]

In 1902 President Theodore Roosevelt sought to make the White House interiors, at least the public rooms, more complementary to the building's late eighteenth-century exterior architecture. This renovation was entrusted to the New York architects McKim, Mead & White, who relied on many fashionable New York suppliers for furniture in a variety of eighteenth- and early nineteenth-century styles. This set a new historical tone and greatly reduced the opportunities for serious decorative change in the twentieth century.

But in keeping with nineteenth-century practice, one great auction of White House property, including many objects that had been provided over the years by local merchants, was held on January 21, 1903:

A large number of relic hunters, second-hand dealers in antiques and private citizens crowded Sloan's [the still-operating C. G. Sloan & Co.] auction rooms on G street today in attendance on the sale of old White House furniture and fixtures discarded in the recent remodeling and refurbishing of the Executive Mansion. The bidding was generally spirited, and most of the articles brought a good price. What those articles lacked in soundness and usefulness was made up to the purchasers in the associations connected with their having been used in the home of many Presidents of the United States.[49]

WILLIAM G. ALLMAN

The Family Dining Room showing an extant mahogany dining table purchased in 1890 from W. H. Houghton & Co. The firm applied a brass plate documenting the circumstances of its service to the White House.

FURNISHING THE EXECUTIVE MANSION

157

1. *Annals of Congress,* 6th Cong., 1799–1801, 1069–70.

2. Ibid., 1068–69.

3. Act of Congress, March 3, 1805, from *Statement of Appropriations and Expenditures from the National Treasury for the District of Columbia from July 16, 1790, to June 30, 1876.*

4. Bill of November 15, 1808, National Archives, General Accounting Office no. 21304, voucher 6, February 3, 1809.

5. Benjamin Henry Latrobe to Dolley Madison, March 22, 1809, Latrobe Papers, Maryland Historical Society.

6. Margaret Brown Klapthor, "Benjamin Latrobe and Dolley Madison Decorate the White House, 1809–1811," *Contributions from the Museum of History and Technology,* bulletin 241, paper 49, Smithsonian Institution, 1965, 161.

7. Latrobe to Dolley Madison, September 8, 1809, Latrobe Papers, Maryland Historical Society; Dolley Madison to Latrobe, September 12, 1809, cited in Talbot Hamlin, *Benjamin Henry Latrobe* (New York: Oxford University Press, 1955), 328–29.

8. "Statement of William Lee . . . ," February 24, 1818, *Congressional Serial no. 10,* no. 143, 15th Cong., 1st sess., March 9, 1818, 3.

9. GAO no. 34714 V-11, November 11, 1815; George McCue, *The Octagon* (Washington: AIA Foundation, 1976), 61.

10. GAO no. 28634 V-25, July 10, 1815; bills of October 23, 1815 to January 17, 1817, V-31, January 22, 1817.

11. "Statement of William Lee," 3.

12. GAO no. 37131 V-3, May 1818; "Statement of William Lee," 5.

13. *Eastern Argus,* Portland, Me., December 2, 1817, quoted in "Clues and Footnotes," ed. Eleanor H. Gustafson, *Antiques* (September 1977), 522.

14. ". . . the Message of the President . . . on the subject of his Public Accounts," *House Reports* no. 79, 18th Cong., 2d sess., December 17, 1818, 182; Anne Castrodale Golovin, "William King, Jr., Georgetown Furniture Maker," *Antiques* (May 1977), 1032–37.

15. *House Reports* no. 79, item 9, July 1, 1818, 146; item 14, June 8, 1818, 148–49; bill of October 18, 1818, GAO no. 43754 V-66, with endorsement of May 4, 1819.

16. William Lee to Samuel Lane, Commissioner of Public Buildings, May 28, 1818, GAO no. 43754; also V-19, June 1, 1818.

WILLIAM G. ALLMAN

17. William Easby to David Baird, June 8, 1851, National Archives, Commissioner of Public Buildings, Letter Book, vol. 10, 1851–53, 95; bill of November 1, 1851, GAO no. 107778, 143, April 29, 1852.

18. "Statement of William Lee," 5.

19. *House Reports* no. 79, item 12, May 20, 1818, 147–48.

20. James Monroe to Congress, *House Reports* no. 79, 131; also Acts of Congress, March 3, 1817, $20,000, April 18, 1818, $30,000, 139.

21. "Statement of William Lee," 4; Act of Congress, May 22, 1826.

22. Transcript of letter, January 5, 1823, Office of the Curator, the White House.

23. National Archives, Records of the House of Representatives, 19th Cong., February 8, 1826; GAO no. 51873 V-73, July 6, 1825; V-41, May 18, 1825; V-8, March 26, 1825; V-5, April 6, 1825; V-7 April 6, 1825.

24. Anne Castrodale Golovin, "Cabinetmakers and Chairmakers of Washington, D.C., 1791–1840," *Antiques* (May 1975), 898–922, quoting *Daily National Intelligencer,* September 2, 1825, and December 22, 1825.

25. GAO no. A-61369 V-39, December 2, 1829; GAO no. 70647 V-4, December 30, 1833; V-3, December 16, 1833; V-2, August 24, 1833.

26. Golovin, "Cabinetmakers," 913, quoting *Daily National Intelligencer,* January 4, 1830.

27. GAO no. 70467 V-D, December 7, 1833; V-E, December 5, 1833.

28. GAO no. 70467 V-1, July 1, 1833.

29. *Speech of Mr. Ogle of Pennsylvania, on the Royal Splendor of the Presidential Palace* (Boston: Weeks, Jordan, 1840).

30. Ibid., 18; William Noland to Hon. Walter Coles, June 25, 1840, National Archives, Office of Public Buildings, Letters Received, vol 30, no. 3002.

31. Purchases of February 23, 1841, and March 23, 1841, GAO no. 87143 V-1, July 24, 1841; Golovin, "Cabinetmakers," 913, quoting *Daily National Intelligencer,* April 5, 1839.

32. Bill of February 26, 1841, GAO no. 81944, June 22, 1841.

33. William Seale, *The President's House: A History* (Washington: White House Historical Association, 1986), 235.

34. GAO no. 105580 V-8, December 30, 1850; GAO no. 107778 V-4, January 17, 1851; GAO no. 51873 V-14, April 18, 1825.

35. GAO no. 136728 V-20, February 2, 1860; GAO no. 136728, February 14, 1860, 160–61.

36. Seale, *President's House,* 382–83, 420; National Archives, Records of the

Office of Public Buildings, 1861–65; Mary Todd Lincoln to Hon. Edward McPherson, December 14, 1863, copy, Office of the Curator, the White House.

37. GAO no. 157178 V-41-48, May 9, 1865; Records of the Office of Public Buildings, 1866–67; GAO no. 169995 V-1, May 3, 1867; GAO no. 173118 V-1, April 3, 1869.

38. Rakeman autobiographical notes, files of the Architect of the Capitol, Records of the House of Representatives, 1869, National Archives.

39. (Pottier & Stymus) Records of the Office of Public Buildings, September 18, 1869, National Archives; (Herter) GAO no. 188179 V-9, October 3, 1872; GAO no. 202494 V-36, January 18, 1876.

40. (Williams) GAO no. 173118 V-8, December 1869, $800 and $750; (Moses) GAO no. 173118 V-3, April 14, 1869, $1,306; GAO no. 18754 V-6, May 24, 1871, $391; GAO no. 192268 V-37, January 15, 1874, $1,479; (Wight) GAO no. 200817 V-204, December 23, 1875, $675.

41. GAO no. 176596 V-15, May 12, 1870.

42. Records of the Office of Public Buildings, Letters Received no. 96, March 23, 1881, National Archives; Commissioner of Public Buildings disbursement summary no. 1, June 30, 1866, V-21, January 31, 1866, National Archives.

43. Seale, *President's House,* 516–17, 533.

44. Records of the Office of Public Buildings, V-60, December 22, 1882, National Archives; (Moses) Records of the Office of Public Buildings, Accounts Received, V-16, January 20, 1883; V-21, July 23, 1883; V-48, August 27, 1883.

45. *Evening Star,* April 13, 1882; *Washington Post,* April 15, 1882.

46. GAO no. 277269 V-24, May 21, 1890; GAO no. 287852 V-1, October 1, 1891, and V-74, December 16, 1891.

47. *Annual Report of the Officer in Charge of Public Buildings and Grounds* (Washington: Government Printing Office, 1901), 3745; Records of the Office of Public Buildings, Accounts Received, V-28, November 1894; V-27, April 1896; V-23, January 27, 1899, National Archives.

48. GAO no. 5366 V-55, July 29, 1897; GAO no. 6491 V-34, August 30, 1897; V-58, November 26, 1897; GAO no. 14493 V-18, October 20, 1899.

49. *Evening Star,* January 21, 1903.

WILLIAM G. ALLMAN

160

SEVEN

The Landscape of the President's House: Garden of Democracy

SUZANNE TURNER

A 1991 PIECE in the *New York Times* proposed that the president rip out the White House lawn and replace it with something more ecologically sound. The author, tongue in cheek, proposed several alternatives: a meadow of native grasses; an organic vegetable garden to feed the poor of Washington; a wetland, restoring a portion of the site to its original condition; or an apple orchard. His favored solution was the orchard, something that would "celebrate our democratic spirit . . . without offending nature."[1]

Intentionally or not, the author's images were evocative of the character of the early White House landscape, which included all these elements. In fact, Pierre-Charles L'Enfant, in a 1791 letter to Jefferson, had noted an apple orchard just back from the ridge where the White House would stand.[2]

The purpose of this paper is not to suggest ripping out the White House lawn but to show how the White House landscape has related to the democratic ideals of the American people throughout its history. If one traces the evolution of the site, as it was laid out and planted, designed and redesigned, one may discover, in essence, the evolution of the nation: from a nation of farmers, working to blend the requirements of husbandry with the ornamental elements of a garden, to an industrial nation, with less pressure to farm and more time for the pursuit of ornamental horticulture, and then to a postindustrial and information-centered nation, more concerned with security and the management and conservation of the landscape than with lavish display.

The landscape in which the President's House began to rise in 1792 was as yet untamed, dotted with old farmsteads, remnant agricultural fields, and orchards, all surrounded by wooden palisades that fenced out roaming animals. Although L'Enfant's plans for the young city of Washington specified axial lines slicing through these farmsteads and the adjacent forests,

"Elevation of the south front of the President's House copied from the design as to be altered in 1807. January 1817, B. H. Latrobe." Latrobe's 1817 elevation of the south front, showing a half-round porch, is labeled as a copy of the drawing made in 1807. Latrobe's drawing for the south portico may have begun as an idea during Jefferson's administration, but probably dates from early in the rebuilding process under Madison.

SUZANNE TURNER

recalling the pageantry of the court of Versailles, when the grounds of the house were finally laid out, the result was the antithesis of earlier European palatial residences. The grounds were simply treated as the grounds of many of the plantations in the surrounding Virginia and Maryland countryside had been. The appendages concomitant with any working farm—kitchen garden, stables, servants' quarters, storerooms—were still necessities for the President's House in 1800.

The landscape was first nothing more than a construction staging ground, littered with unpainted temporary workers' housing, brickyards and kilns, stacks of stone and timber, the cookhouse, and pits for brick tempering and pit-sawing.[3] Benjamin Stoddert, secretary of the navy, was concerned that John Adams, the first occupant of the White House, be as comfortable as possible when he moved in, and in January 1800 he wrote to William Thornton, the architect of the Capitol:

> It will give the president and Mrs. Adams great satisfaction if you
> will plan, and cause to be executed, something like a garden, at the
> north side of the President's House. . . . I mean something . . . en-
> closed with open railing. The ground should not be levelled—but
> Trees should be planted at once, so as to make it an agreeable place
> to walk in, even this summer. . . . Is there a stable—a carriage
> House—too is necessary.[4]

Mrs. Stoddert recorded in her diary that Secretary Stoddert had sent "his ground plan of the President's House" to Thornton, but no further trace of the plan survives.[5] When Adams made his inspection of the still-unfinished White House in June 1800, one of his primary concerns was that there was no vegetable garden. In response, a garden was planted "on the northeast side of the White House, probably in the fenced part of the old stone yard."[6] When Adams moved in five months later, the house was still surrounded by the mire and disorder of the construction site.

Thomas Jefferson's interest and skill in landscape gardening is well

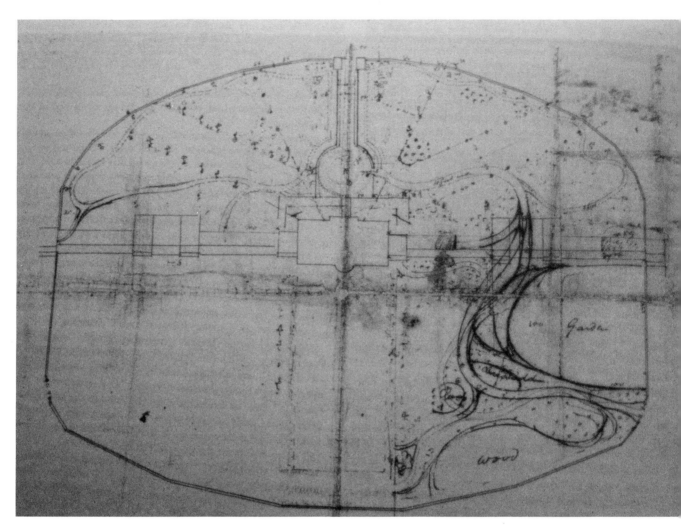

A drawing of the outline of the grounds of the President's House as developed between 1808 and 1818. The dotted and faint lines seem to indicate conditions existing at the time of the drawing; solid heavy lines in the right portion appear to be studies for changes to be made upon the removal of the stable to the east of the President's House. This drawing, probably by Jefferson, was for the expansion of the house as well as for the landscaping and fencing of the White House grounds, ca. 1804. By this plan Jefferson reduced the approximately sixty-acre White House grounds to a high-walled yard of some five acres, leaving a public common on the north and meadows and abandoned marshes on the south. On the north he has proposed allées of trees. The east and west wings, or "terraces," are outlined as he intended them, extending to the executive office buildings, with large structures interrupting them midway.

SUZANNE TURNER

documented, and it is not surprising that this self-taught architect and landscape designer would want to place his imprint on the landscape he would occupy for eight years. With Benjamin Latrobe, his surveyor of public buildings, Jefferson made attempts to expand the architectural space of the White House by adding wings on both sides. A stable and cowshed were built on the Treasury side, with a "bower-like, one-story structure on the opposite side for offices." The office wing housed a meat house, a wine cellar, coal and wood sheds, and privies,[7] in a plan reminiscent of the treatment of the service wings at Monticello (1804–8), and the biaxial geometry of his retreat, Poplar Forest (1806–16).[8] Fowl and goats were housed in wooden sheds left over from the construction of the house, and cows grazed on the grounds.[9]

It is during Jefferson's term that we have the first evidence of a landscape plan for the White House grounds. In 1807 Latrobe, probably under Jefferson's supervision, drew the first known landscape plan for the grounds, in a sketch that designated areas as "garden," "clump," "wood," and "park." C. Allan Brown, a Jeffersonian landscape scholar, describes the plan as an "uncommon union of straight lines and serpentine curves."[10] It is as if L'Enfant's imperialistic geometry and Jefferson's fascination with the picturesque had had as their point of intersection the front door of the White House. Curved carriage roads and pedestrian paths wound among groups of plantings and across axial allées of trees. Although the plan was incomplete and very much a working sketch, it suggested the basic form that the south grounds would eventually take after the implementation of Downing's 1851 plan.

The origin of the two mounds flanking the south grounds, which serve to separate the house and its grounds from the public's view, is controversial. Whether these were proposed by Jefferson or built from excavated fill in 1855,[11] the notion of using mounds in this manner was apparently a familiar one in Jefferson's time. Similar mounds flank the entrance to the carriage road at Mount Vernon.

With the administration of John Quincy Adams we begin to have words and pictures that help us visualize the appearance of the White House landscape more clearly. In 1825 Adams appointed John Ousley as his gardener, and together the two set about making improvements on the grounds. The most thorough description is from Adams's own memoirs:

In this small garden of less than two acres that are forest and fruit trees, shrubs, hedges, esculent vegetables, kitchen and medicinal

The White House, unsigned painting by Anthony St. John Baker, ca. 1826–27, tipped into the author's own *Mémoires d'un voyageur qui se repose,* now in the Huntington Library, San Marino, California. This small watercolor shows the White House and its landscape of numerous animal and storage sheds, workmen's shanties, muddy streets, and wooden palings around what might be an orchard in the foreground, Jefferson's stone wall, and the ruggedness of the terrain south of the site.

SUZANNE TURNER

herbs, hot-house plants, flowers, and weeds to the amount, I conjecture, of at least one thousand. . . . I ask the name of every plant I see.

Ousley, the gardener, knows almost all of them by their botanical names. . . . From the small patch where the medicinal herbs stand together I plucked this morning leaves of balm and hyssop, marjoram, mint, rue, sage, tansy, tarragon and wormwood.[12]

Ousley and Adams increased the size of the vegetable and flower gardens to approximately ten thousand square feet and laid out "an enclosure in the yard westward of the house, containing between one and two acres of ground for a nursery."[13] It was a time of intense interest in botany and horticulture, and Adams was squarely at the center of this endeavor. With Ousley he experimented with the cultivation of American tree species, and in the nursery they planted the seeds of hundreds of native American trees, including oaks, chestnuts, and black walnuts.[14] They were looking ahead to a time when there would be an urgent need to conserve the timber resources of the new nation.

It was under the administration of Millard Fillmore that perhaps the most definitive step would be taken to establish the character of the grounds of the President's House. In 1851 Fillmore commissioned the renowned landscape designer Andrew Jackson Downing to lay out the Mall and the grounds south of the White House. According to Downing's plan, the park of the President's House was one of six related gardens that would form a network of landscapes, weaving together the Capitol, the Mall, and the White House. The plan is difficult to read, but proposes a great circle on the south grounds, and two clumps of trees in the position of the two present mounds.[15] Downing tragically drowned in 1852, on the first leg of his journey to Washington to present his final plans. The drawings for the White House gardens were lost in the accident.[16] He left as a legacy his prolific popular writings on landscape design, the designs of numerous

Young trees dot the south lawn in the earliest photograph of the White House, ca. 1846.

Facing page: A view of the interior of the White House greenhouse in 1858.

SUZANNE TURNER

estates in the Hudson River Valley, and the comprehensive plan that would guide the future of the city's public open spaces. Frederick Law Olmsted, who would soon design Central Park in New York, urged the implementation of Downing's plan for the Mall after his untimely death, saying that it was "the only essay made under our government in landscape gardening."[17]

In 1858, under James Buchanan, a greenhouse was removed from the White House grounds to make way for the west extension of the Treasury Building, and a new conservatory and stable were constructed on the foundation of the west terrace. An account from 1858 describes the glasshouse:

> As you enter the conservatory itself it seems almost like penetrating the luxurious fragrance of some South American island, so warm

Mrs. McKinley in the Conservatory of the Executive Mansion, Washington.
Copyright 1900 by Underwood & Underwood.

In this stereographic pair of pictures Ida Saxton McKinley, in a ball gown with a long train, sits in the first court of the conservatory, just beyond the glass doors from the State Dining Room, ca. 1898. Mrs. McKinley was small and pale and, having lost two children in their infancy, she suffered dark periods of depression. Except for her love of the roses in the conservatory, she took little interest in the White House. The gardener, Henry Pfister, expanded the collections in the rose house and made arrangements for the First Lady every day she was in residence.

Facing page: The east garden of the White House, looking west, ca. 1925. Ellen Axson Wilson, Woodrow Wilson's first wife and an avid gardener herself, had invited the celebrated landscape designer Beatrix Farrand in 1913 to make plans for the east garden. The garden was trim and green and architectural in character; a lawn framed by undulating lines of boxwood had at its center a rectangular lily pond, with beds and borders lavishly planted in flowers. Although the project for the east garden was under way, it had not been completed when Mrs. Wilson died in the summer of 1914.

SUZANNE TURNER

and odiferous is the atmosphere. . . . Here you may see orange trees, and a lemon tree . . . rows of prickly cactus of every size and shape . . . camellia japonica, delicate spirea, ardisia, and poinsettia.[18]

In 1934 Franklin D. Roosevelt invited Olmsted's son and successor in the practice, Frederick Law Olmsted, Jr., to redesign the White House grounds. The younger Olmsted's reputation in Washington was already well established: he had, along with Charles McKim and Daniel Burnham, planned the Mall in 1901. Olmsted was critical of the condition of the grounds and placed a high priority on those historic elements that were basic to the site's integrity, particularly the vista to the south. Olmsted's introduction to his report states his attitudes best:

> The White House grounds, in spite of certain defects . . . are characterized by many long-established landscape qualities of great dignity and appropriateness. It is of the utmost importance to perpetuate these qualities . . . to strengthen and perfect them instead of obscuring or weakening them.
>
> Some of these admirable qualities inherited from the past are obvious; some have already been obscured by past deliberate or accidental alterations. In order to understand them clearly and provide a sound basis for continuity of purpose in management a thorough study of the landscape history of the grounds is necessary.[19]

He hired Morley Williams, who had worked on the history and restoration of the Mount Vernon landscape, to compile a chronology of the events in the site's evolution. Olmsted's 1935 report stands today as a model for the stewardship of a historic landscape, using a methodology that has become commonplace in professional practice only in the last fifteen or so years. It is this report that today remains the guiding manual for decisions on the White House grounds.

SUZANNE TURNER

This brief survey of the more significant events and personalities in the history of the White House landscape provides enough of the story to begin to assess the meaning of this landscape. One question is central to a deeper understanding of this national icon: to what degree do the successive designs for the White House grounds represent landscapes distinct from the traditions of England and France? In other words, to what degree do they reflect the creation of a tradition that is uniquely American—one that bespeaks democracy?

James Madison, writing in 1787, suggested that in the development of the capital city of the young democracy, there would be a balance between precedent and invention:

> Is it not the glory of the people of America, that whilst they have
> paid a decent regard to the opinions of former times and other na-
> tions, they have not suffered a blind veneration for antiquity, for cus-
> tom, or for names, to overrule the suggestions of their own good
> sense, the knowledge of their own situation, and the lessons of their
> own experience?[20]

Madison meant the situation and experience of a farmer or planter—the experience of the majority of early American settlers and of early American presidents as well. These early leaders were men of the soil, and quite accomplished in this occupation. Although both Washington and Jefferson developed sophisticated landscape design statements on their own estates, their primary occupation was with planting cash crops.

If we look at the popular gardening literature of the early nation, we see what issues occupied the minds of the rural farmer. In 1790 Samuel Deane published *The New England Farmer; or, Georgical Dictionary*, a manual of husbandry as applied to that region. He wrote about the place of agriculture in the new nation:

> The writer has had more zeal and courage in attempting to promote
> improvements in agriculture, since the happy termination of the late

struggle for independence than before. Our holding the rank of a free and independent nation allows us to consider the country as indisputably our own, and ourselves as monarchs over our farms. . . .

But the most forcible reason for our cultivating this art is the indispensable necessity of it, to enable us to live as becomes an independent people.[21]

The image of Americans as monarchs over their farms seemed apt to describe the energies and attitudes of the first generations of Americans, and the first presidents as well. Deane's book concentrated on the essentials of farm management, and made only passing mention of horticultural topics. There was no list of flowers or herbal plants. Though he used the term *gardening*, his definition implied the kitchen garden, John Adams's first concern at the White House. Deane urged his readers to observe the trees around them and included a list of nineteen indigenous trees and shrubs, with their flowering and foliation dates. More than anything else, Deane's volume indicates the desire for Americans to have information on the specifics of farming on their new continent, and on the role of farming as a means of independent living.[22]

In 1804 John Gardiner and David Hepburn published in Washington, D.C., *The American Gardener*, the first American gardening publication to broaden its scope and deal with the flower garden.[23] The authors provided month-by-month information on the kitchen garden, flower garden, vineyard, nursery, hopyard, greenhouse, and hothouse. Listed as subscribers to this publication were fifty-six members of Congress, as well as President Thomas Jefferson, Vice President Aaron Burr, Secretary of State James Madison, and the secretaries of war, the treasury, and the navy.[24] Certainly the appearance in this book of the same kind of comprehensive approach to gardening as was practiced by Jefferson, involving ornamental as well as vegetable gardens, attests to a time when Americans were secure in their agricultural future and anxious to dabble in gardening for pleasure.

A photograph giving a south view, with sheep, during the Wilson administration.

Two years after the publication of Gardiner and Hepburn's *American Gardener*, Bernard M'Mahon published *The American Gardener's Calendar*,[25] considered by many as the "first really serviceable American horticultural work and definitive gardening book," which was to undergo eleven editions by 1857. In 1841 Downing recognized the work as the "only American work . . . which treats directly of landscape gardening."[26] Although the tenets of romantic landscape gardening would not be introduced to the American public on a broad scale until the publication of Downing's *Treatise on the Theory and Practice of Landscape Gardening Adapted to North America* in 1841, M'Mahon suggested design ideas that were of the

English aesthetic, the aesthetic that would dominate the look of the White House landscape throughout its evolution. Downing's genius for publishing would later cause these ideals of naturalistic landscape gardening to be embraced not only by the elite but also by the middle class, aspiring to improve their home grounds. Through him these ideas became available to every American.

Downing's explanation of his threefold intentions for his design for the Mall clearly sounds the democratic overtones of his approach. He wrote to President Fillmore in 1851 that he wished first to form a national park that "would be an ornament to the Capital of the United States." Second, he hoped "to give an example of the natural style of landscape gardening which may have an influence on the general taste of the country." Finally, he hoped to form a "public museum of living trees and shrubs where every person visiting Washington would become familiar with the habits and growth of all the hardy trees."[27] Downing was grounded in agrarian values and believed in the power of landscape to form the attitudes of Americans.[28] His desire for the general public to understand and embrace the natural style demonstrated his commitment to the ideals of a democratic republic.

In the natural style lay the opportunity to leave behind the controlling geometries of absolute political rule, and to explore and celebrate the visual quality of the American landscape in all its uniqueness. The look of pastoral scenery fit a nation confident in its future, a nation pushing its boundaries to the far west. The natural aesthetic worked for the White House, for it spoke to the American people in a language that they could understand and adopt as their own. It represented the freedom of open space, the quality that most distinguished the new land from that of Europe. The landscape of the White House that Downing envisioned gave an illusion of space that went on forever in many directions, across the river, and beyond the horizon.

In 1780, as a diplomat in Paris, John Adams had been emphatic about what he felt the priorities of a new democratic nation should be:

SUZANNE TURNER

The rural Scenes around this Town are charming. The public Walks, Gardens, &c. are extreamly beautifull. The Gardens of the Palais Royal, the Gardens of the Tuilleries, are very fine. The Place de Louis 15, the Place Vendome or Place de Louis 14, the Place victoire, the Place royal, are fine Squares, ornamented with very magnificent statues. . . .

   It is not indeed the fine Arts, which our Country requires. The Usefull, the mechanic Arts, are those which We have occasion for in a young Country, as yet simple and not far advanced in Luxury. . . . The Science of Government it is my Duty to study, more than all other Sciences; . . . I must study Politicks and War that my sons may have liberty to study Mathematicks and Philosophy, Geography, natural History, Naval Architecture, navigation, Commerce and Agriculture, in order to give their Children a right to study Painting, Poetry, Musick, Architecture, Statuary, Tapestry and Porcelaine. Adieu.[29]

Adams was critical of the excesses he saw in Europe, and intent that the United States not fall into the same pattern. He felt that the nation must first be secured before its citizens should explore the arts. The development of the White House landscape parallels Adams's thinking about the order of refinement in American culture, beginning as a landscape of utility, with emphasis on food production and the stabling of animals, and eventually becoming a landscape of aesthetics, embellished with flowers, ornamental shrubs, and trees. President John Quincy Adams followed his father's directive and, because of the labors of his father's generation, was able to pursue the fine arts, to use landscape design and horticulture to embody his own personal philosophy.

   John Adams's vision for the American landscape went far beyond an apple orchard; he saw for the generations of Americans that would follow him a way of life that would spring "fresh from the hearts and judgments of an honest and enlightened people."[30] He must surely have envisioned a landscape for the President's House that would possess clarity of purpose, simplicity, and dignity, and that might indeed one day be called the "garden of democracy." The words that Adams used to describe the Constitution of the United States are strangely fitting to describe the White House landscape and the process that created it: "An experiment, better adapted to the genius, character, situation, and relations of this nation and country, than any which had ever been proposed or suggested."[31]

NOTES

1. Michael Pollan, "Abolish the White House Lawn," *The New York Times,* May 5, 1991.

2. William Seale, *The President's House* (Washington: White House Historical Association/Abrams, 1986), 3n8, 1069 (L'Enfant to Jefferson [Georgetown], March 11, 1791, L'Enfant Papers, Library of Congress).

3. Ibid., 66.

4. Stoddert to William Thornton, January 20, 1800, William Thornton Papers, Library of Congress, as cited by Eleanor M. McPeck, "The President's Garden: An Account of the White House Gardens from 1800 to the Present," unpublished report, August 1971, 5–6, in the collection of the Office of the Curator, the White House.

5. "Diary of Mrs. William Thornton," March 20, 1800, Library of Congress, as cited in McPeck, "President's Garden," 6.

6. Stoddert to William Thornton, Philadelphia, January 20 and 30, 1800, William Thornton Papers, Library of Congress, as cited by Seale, *President's House,* 78, 1078n100.

7. Herbert R. Collins, "The White House Stables and Garages," reprinted from the Records of the Columbia Historical Society of Washington, D.C., 1963–65.

8. C. Allan Brown, "Poplar Forest: The Mathematics of an Ideal Villa," *Journal of Garden History* 10 (1990):121–23.

9. Seale, *President's House,* 102.

10. Brown, "Poplar Forest," 123.

11. Correspondence between John Blake, Commissioner of Public Buildings, and Secretary of the Interior McClelland, July 6, July 12, July 14, 1855, included in file "Mounds" in the Office of the Curator, the White House, documents the

plan to build mounds from the earth excavated for the foundation of the Treasury Building.

12. John Quincy Adams, *Memoirs of John Quincy Adams,* ed. Charles Francis Adams (Philadelphia: Lippincott, 1875), 7:288.

13. Jack Shepherd, "Seeds of the Presidency: The Capitol Schemes of John Quincy Adams," *Horticulture* (January 1983), 40.

14. In vol. 1 of the *Adams Family Correspondence,* ed. L. H. Butterfield and Marc Friedlander (Cambridge, Mass.: Belknap Press, 1973), a line drawing of an acorn and oak leaves with the motto "Alteri seculo" depicts a seal cut for John Quincy Adams after 1830. The motto is from Caecilius Statius as quoted by Cicero in the First Tusculan Disputation: *Serit arbores quae alteri seculo prosint* ("He plants trees for the benefit of later generations") (1:vi).

15. Olmsted Brothers, Landscape Architects, "Report to the President of the United States on Improvements and Policy of Maintenance for the Executive Mansion Grounds," October 1935, Collection of the Office of the Curator, the White House.

16. Seale, *President's House,* 300.

17. Frederick Law Olmsted, "Park Improvement Papers: A Series of Seventeen Papers Relating to the Improvement of the Park System of the District of Columbia," Washington, D.C., 1902, as cited in Therese O'Malley, "'A Public Museum of Trees': Mid-Nineteenth Century Plans for the Mall," in *The Mall in Washington, 1791–1991,* ed. Richard Longstreth (Washington: The National Gallery of Art, 1991), 73.

18. Leslie, "Account of Miss Lane's Retreat," 1858, as cited in McPeck, "President's Garden," 31.

19. Olmsted Brothers, "Report to the President," 1.

20. James Madison, *The Federalist; or, The New Constitution,* no. 14, 2d ed., by Alexander Hamilton, James Madison, and John Jay, ed. Max Beloff (New York: Basil Blackwell, 1987), 66.

21. Samuel Deane, *The New England Farmer; or, Georgical Dictionary: Containing a Compendious Account of the Ways and Methods in Which the Important Art of Husbandry, in All Its Various Branches, Is, or May Be, Practised to the Greatest Advantage in This Country,* 2d ed. (Worcester, Mass.: Isaiah Thomas, 1797).

22. Brenda Bullion, "Early American Farming and Gardening Literature: 'Adapted to the Climates and Seasons of the United States,'" *Journal of Garden History* 12 (1992): 32–33.

23. Ibid., 37.

24. John Gardiner and David Hepburn, *The American Gardener: Containing Ample Directions for Working a Kitchen Garden, Every Month in the Year; and Copious Instructions for the Cultivation of Flower Gardens, Vineyards, Nurseries, Hop-Yards, Green Houses, and Hot Houses* (Washington: Samuel H. Smith, 1804).

25. Bernard M'Mahon. *The American Gardener's Calendar: Adapted to the Climates and Seasons of the United States* (Philadelphia: B. Graves, 1806).

26. Bullion, "Early American Farming," 38.

27. Andrew Jackson Downing, "Explanatory Notes to Accompany the Plan for Improving the Public Grounds at Washington, D.C.," March 3, 1851, Records of the Commissioners of Public Buildings, Letters Received, RG 42, LR, vol. 32, National Archives, as cited in O'Malley, "'A Public Museum of Trees,'" 66.

28. O'Malley, "'A Public Museum of Trees,'" passim.

29. John Adams to Abigail Adams, Paris, post May 12, 1780, in *Adams Family Correspondence* 3:341–42.

30. John Adams, "Inaugural Address of the President of the United States," in *Letters of John Adams Addressed to His Wife* (Boston: Little, Brown, 1841), 277.

31. Ibid., 276.

BIBLIOGRAPHY

Adams, John. *Letters of John Adams Addressed to His Wife*. Boston: Little, Brown, 1841.

Adams, John Quincy. *Memoirs of John Quincy Adams*. Edited by Charles Francis Adams. Vol. 7. Philadelphia: Lippincott, 1875.

Beloff, Max, editor. *The Federalist; or, The New Constitution*. By Alexander Hamilton, James Madison, and John Jay. 2d ed. New York: Basil Blackwell, 1987.

Brown, C. Allan. "Poplar Forest: The Mathematics of an Ideal Villa." *Journal of Garden History* 10, (1990):121–23.

Bullion, Brenda. "Early American Farming and Gardening Literature: 'Adapted to the Climates and Seasons of the United States.'" *Journal of Garden History* 12 (1992): 29–51.

Butterfield, L. H., editor. *The Adams Papers*. Vol. 1. Cambridge, Mass.: Belknap Press, 1963.

Collins, Herbert C. "The White House Stables and Garages." Reprinted from the Records of the Columbia Historical Society of Washington, D.C., 1963–65.

Deane, Samuel. *The New England Farmer; or, Georgical Dictionary: Containing a*

Compendious Account of the Ways and Methods in Which the Important Art of Husbandry, in All Its Various Branches, Is, or May Be, Practised to the Greatest Advantage in This Country. 2d ed. Worcester, Mass.: Isaiah Thomas, 1797.

Gardiner, John, and David Hepburn. *The American Gardener: Containing Ample Directions for Working a Kitchen Garden, Every Month in the Year; and Copious Instructions for the Cultivation of Flower Gardens, Vineyards, Nurseries, Hop-Yards, Green Houses, and Hot Houses.* Washington: Samuel H. Smith, 1804.

Greenberg, Allan. "L'Enfant, Washington, and the Plan of the Capital," *Antiques* (July 1991): 112–23.

McEwan, Barbara. *White House Landscapes: Horticultural Achievements of American Presidents.* New York: Walker, 1992.

McPeck, Eleanor. "The President's Garden: An Account of the White House Gardens from 1800 to the Present." Unpublished report, August 1971.

Olmsted Brothers, Landscape Architects. "Report to the President of the United States on Improvements and Policy of Maintenance for the Executive Mansion Grounds." October 1935.

O'Malley, Therese. "'A Public Museum of Trees': Mid-Nineteenth Century Plans for the Mall." In *The Mall in Washington, 1797–1991,* edited by Richard Longstreth. Washington: The National Gallery of Art, 1991.

Pollan, Michael. "Abolish the White House Lawn." *New York Times,* May 5, 1991.

Seale, William. Personal files.

———. *The President's House.* 2 vols. Washington: The White House Historical Association, National Geographic Society, and Harry N. Abrams, 1986.

———. *The White House: The History of an American Idea.* Washington: American Institute of Architects Press/The White House Historical Association, 1992.

Shepherd, Jack. "Seeds of the Presidency: The Capitol Schemes of John Quincy Adams," *Horticulture* (January 1983), 38–47.

— EIGHT —

McKim's Renovations: American Renaissance and Imperial Presidency

RICHARD GUY WILSON

UNDER the patronage of President Theodore Roosevelt, Charles Follen McKim transformed the White House not just physically but also symbolically, creating a new iconography for the United States. McKim's work at the White House in 1902 converted the residence of the president of the United States into a ritualistic setting for pomp and pageantry. This change personified a new American political order, an "American Renaissance" as it was frequently called, as the United States increasingly took on an imperial cast in both politics and the arts.

This new vision of America could be observed in McKim's new Blue Room. In 1899, during the McKinley administration, E. S. Yergason of New York, with the assistance of the local furniture and upholstery house W. B. Moses & Sons, redecorated the Blue Room. Yergason had slightly updated the 1881–82 redecoration that Louis Comfort Tiffany had carried out during the presidency of Chester A. Arthur. Essentially a busy combination of conflicting patterns, colors, and forms, Yergason claimed his Blue Room as an example of "colonial" decoration, but it appeared more like a refuge

Before and after: above, the Blue Room is shown ca. 1900, as decorated by W. B. Moses & Sons; below is the Blue Room after McKim's renovation of 1902 discarded the excesses of the Victorian era.

Greenhouses on the roof of the west terrace, ca. 1900. The first greenhouse was built in 1857 by President James Buchanan, who admired the Crystal Palace while living in England. The plant-filled conservatory was large, covering nearly all the west wing, and built of wood, not the iron originally proposed. During the administration of Andrew Johnson, on a morning in January 1867, the conservatory was destroyed by fire and the losses were heavy. The ruins were cleared away before the end of the winter so that construction of a new fireproof greenhouse of cast-iron frame could begin. The new conservatory was almost twice the size of the one that had burned. Grant in his administration ordered several additions to the greenhouse, expanding it southward. The greenhouses, referred to collectively as the conservatory, became a cherished retreat for the presidents. Hayes dressed them up by rearranging the interiors with broad walks and iron benches, making them more spacious for entertaining large groups of guests. But the architect McKim detested the long range of greenhouses as reminders of Victorian utilitarianism and vulgarity, and had them torn down in the 1902 renovation.

RICHARD GUY WILSON

from a jumble sale with its melee of decorative schemes. The chairs were at least twenty years out of date and were combined with a gigantic seating unit that resembled a mushroom, which Edith Wharton (with Ogden Codman) had contemptuously described in *The Decoration of Houses* (1897) as "modern upholsterer" furniture, fit only for a "lunatic's cell."[1] Garlands dripped and smothered every surface. In contrast, the new Blue Room by McKim exuded architectural unity. McKim created what one writer called a "restoration plus," choosing an Empire-Napoleonic style from around 1818 that represented the noble past of the room. The furniture (white enamel with gilt trim), the mantel, the chandelier, the draperies were appropriately subservient to the architectonic character, the oval shape. McKim covered the walls with a dark blue corded silk with a small Greek key border at the top and the bottom; no large obtrusive patterns here. The directoire chairs by Leon Marcotte and Company of New York were covered in a deep blue lampas with a bright basket-and-flower motif supplied by New York's leading fabric house, F. Schumacher & Co.[2] McKim's transformed Blue Room illustrates the "great cleaning up" that took place across the country during the turn of the century as a refined classicism replaced Victorian clutter and bric-a-brac, which were banished to attics and servant's quarters.

On the exterior as well McKim restored and redefined the image of the White House. He swept away the numerous accretions, such as the iron lanterns that (Charles Moore, the majordomo of Washington aesthetics, claimed) "degraded" the columns of the front portico, the "clumsy" iron fence ornamented with gilded balls, and the "perverted" greenhouses built on Latrobe's west terrace, which smashed into the main house like an "end-on railway collision."[3] McKim added the West (or office) Wing, removing the president's offices from the house itself. He restored the East Wing, making it the new entrance. Similarly, the grounds were newly landscaped, the wide asphalt driveway shrunk, while on the east side Edith Wharton, a cousin and close friend of the president's wife, Edith Roosevelt, assisted in designing a new formal garden that followed the lines of Mount Vernon.[4] The tenor of Charles Moore's language indicates the polemical nature of McKim's work at the White House, for not everybody approved. Some individuals, both critics and politicians, claimed the restoration was too expensive, too royal, and too inaccurate, but to McKim's supporters, he had returned the White House to its origins as a great Georgian mansion with its roots in the eternal world of classicism.[5] With the White House remodeling McKim transformed it into a stage set for a new imperial America, the heir of western civilization. Instead of being a miscellany of interiors and furniture, a large middle-class house where, in typical American helter-skelter fashion, incongruous additions were made as necessities dictated (similar to a farmstead), now the White House was the center of sophistication, quite clearly the residence of a world leader. It exuded confidence; its interiors and exteriors were appropriate to the new expectations that the presidency of Theodore Roosevelt set, in which America strode the international stage. The story of McKim's White House remodeling is complicated, and although writers and historians have recounted the essential facts, the implications of the new symbolism and iconography has seldom been addressed.[6]

Theodore Roosevelt's presidency marked a major shift in American politics, not simply from the point of international power and influence, but at home as well, for with him the chief executive assumed new status and position, no longer just an equal with Congress, but now first among the branches.[7] And with this transformation the White House changed as well; in October 1901, Roosevelt officially changed its name from the prosaic Executive Mansion to the White House, indicating that the house possessed venerability. No longer was it just where the chief executive resided, but instead the building had its own name and personality; it embodied American principles, and great accomplishments were expected of its occupants.[8] The transformation the White House underwent in 1902 is fundamental to the twentieth-century view of the building, for McKim quite clearly sympa-

McKim's East Wing and east entrance of the White House as completed in 1902. Although Roosevelt's extreme distaste for Jefferson was well known ("the most incapable Executive that ever filled the presidential chair"), McKim made quite an issue of rebuilding the East Wing on Jefferson's original foundations. Jefferson, the third president, viewed the East and West Wings as part of a much larger plan to unite the residence with executive buildings to each side. This was to refine the towering, hulking White House by giving it a strong horizontal base, and to provide convenient, covered walkways linked by the vaulted corridor in the basement, as he was doing at Monticello. By shifting service functions into the west end of the building, McKim made way on the east side for several rooms and the social and appointments entrance to the White House.

MCKIM'S RENOVATIONS

Edith Carow Roosevelt, painted by Théobald Chartran, 1902. While his early reputation was made as a creator of historical paintings, the French artist Chartran turned his attention to portraits in the mid-1880s, which brought him important American commissions; he became one of the most fashionable international portraitists. This handsome portrait of Mrs. Theodore Roosevelt is testimony to his skill and his combination of tradition and modernity. The wife of the president posed for this portrait in the colonial garden; the south portico in the background has been repositioned by the artist for pictorial effect. Despite the black coat and splendid feathered hat, the painting is filled with light; Edith Roosevelt's biographer felt that "the pose characteristically combined informality with regality and the calm that was always Edith's most noted attribute." The completed portrait never left the White House; in a letter to Charles McKim in 1902, who was then engaged in a major renovation of the White House, Edith Roosevelt asked the architect to "put all the ladies of the White House, including myself, in the down-stairs corridor. . . . It could then be called the picture gallery."

RICHARD GUY WILSON

thized with Roosevelt's goals; indeed, it might be said he anticipated them and provided the appropriate setting for Roosevelt's new imperial presidency. The new iconography that was presented at the White House comes out of late nineteenth-century culture and the American Renaissance that McKim had helped to create.[9]

The defining event of late nineteenth-century American culture was the World's Columbian Exposition in Chicago of 1893. Here on the shores of Lake Michigan in two short years a group of architects, painters, sculptors, and their financial backers had created an ensemble that spoke of the United States as an heir of the great Western classical tradition. So lofty were the goals of the architects who planned the so-called White City that Augustus Saint-Gaudens, the sculptor, described their deliberations as "the greatest meeting of artists since the fifteenth century!"[10] Although the effect of the Chicago exposition would be felt in many ways, it most directly affected the physical shape of the American city. Momentous changes occurred as new plazas and boulevards were created and new buildings and monuments in revivified classical idioms arose. For many people, both Americans and Europeans, it appeared as if a rebirth had taken place: the country was transformed with major new public buildings, large-scale public art in the form of murals and statues, new city plans, large mansions for the wealthy, apartment blocks, and major commercial structures.

Many individuals, from architects and artists to critics and politicians, used the term *American Renaissance* to indicate the artistic transformation taking place in the United States. For many people it appeared that the spirit which had formed the Renaissance in Italy in the fifteenth and sixteenth centuries was the "rough model," as Bernard Berenson explained, "after which ours is being fashioned."[11] The American Renaissance, although cosmopolitan in its sources, possessed an intense nationalistic spirit; its creators wanted to create the grand backdrop against which the rituals of a great civilization could take place. Prime Minister William Gladstone of England had claimed that "Europe may already see in North America an immediate successor in the march of civilization"; and for many Americans the question arose over what was the appropriate appearance for this new civilization.[12]

Charles McKim of the New York architectural firm McKim, Mead & White had been one of the leaders in Chicago, and in both his public work such as the Boston Public Library (1887–95) and private houses such as the colonial revival H. A. C. Taylor House in Newport, Rhode Island (1883–85), McKim had helped establish classicism as the appropriate basis for American art and architecture. In 1894, fresh from the success of the fair, he founded the American School of Architecture in Rome; a few years later McKim changed its name and mission into the American Academy in Rome. Young architects, painters, and sculptors were to go to Rome to study the "splendid standards of Classic and Renaissance Art" and, as McKim claimed, "delve, bring back and adapt to conditions here, a groundwork on which to build."[13] To McKim, classicism embodied a generic approach to design that was expressed in the individual regional or national styles such as Florentine Italian Renaissance, Palladian, French Louis XIV, or American Georgian; all were part of a great family tree.

In Washington, D.C., the most obvious manifestations of this new American self-consciousness came in the large mansions erected along Sixteenth, Connecticut, and Massachusetts avenues, the plenitude of public sculptures, the Senate Parks (or McMillan) Commission, and the remodeling of the White House. Charles McKim had served on the McMillan Commission from 1901 to 1902, along with Daniel Burnham, Frederick Law Olmsted, Jr., and Augustus Saint-Gaudens. McKim became the dominant artistic voice on the commission, creating the scheme that swept away all the nineteenth-century accretions to the Mall (as was also happening on the interiors of houses), and reasserted Major Pierre-Charles L'Enfant's concept of a great central open space, though now to be terminated by the Lincoln Memorial and a Pantheon to national heroes (which became the Jefferson Memorial in the 1930s). At the initial presentation of the models and plans

The architect Charles Follen McKim (1847–1909), about the time he renovated the White House in 1902. President Theodore Roosevelt put McKim in charge of remaking the Victorianized White House into a neoclassical one, to suit his own new image as a modern president. The revival of neoclassicism was a movement to discipline the licentiousness and capriciousness of the late nineteenth century, a felt need for simplicity and order in reaction to the very different qualities admired in the high Victorian period. McKim rethought the White House in every particular and decided to take the house back to what it had been originally—which meant he could remove all later additions at will. McKim's massive overhaul was to reach for a more stately, ceremonial residence to suit the new presidency—and, indeed, the flamboyant president himself.

MCKIM'S RENOVATIONS

to Congress, the president, and his cabinet at the Corcoran Gallery of Art on January 15, 1902, Roosevelt initially felt critical, but then as he "caught the full import of the treatment," as Charles Moore, the secretary of the commission, recounted, "he became enthusiastic."[14] McKim was not simply the leading architect in the country, but one whose goals were similar to the president's. A symbiosis existed between Roosevelt and McKim: the United States was a world leader and consequently required the appropriate architectural setting.

Theodore Roosevelt, both as a member of his elite social class and as a politician (especially in comparison to his predecessors of the previous thirty years), possessed an unusually refined aesthetic sense. He understood that art, including architecture, meant more than overwhelming opulence—or conspicuous consumption—as was common with the art purchases and the interiors of his wealthy contemporaries. Roosevelt believed that architecture meant more than simply dispensing favors to political supporters or conveying a hackney message concerning power; rather, there were gradations of quality in buildings, and the well-designed structure could inspire as well as control. Roosevelt counted among his friends John La Farge, Saint-Gaudens, and McKim. Under Roosevelt's patronage, Saint-Gaudens and his associates redesigned American coinage, and the Bureau of Engraving and Printing produced the classic stamp stock of 1908. As president, Roosevelt supported the employment of distinguished architects to design government buildings.[15]

At the White House McKim achieved two goals: he saved it, and his restoration made it into a symbol of American cultural aspirations. For a number of years the White House had been under siege as proposals were put forth either to relocate it to other sites, such as Meridian Hill, or to expand the building—such as Colonel Theodore Bingham's gargantuan wings, which would have smothered it.[16] Through his work on the McMillan Commission McKim recognized the symbolic importance of the location of the president's house. Through Charles Moore's researches McKim appreciated the historical associations of the building and equally that it was a building of distinguished architectural character, the product of two great designers, Hoban and Latrobe. Perhaps self-serving, and yet with conviction, Moore recounted a June night in 1902 when he and McKim after dinner at the White House strolled through the grounds and he asked McKim: "'Among the great houses that have been built during recent years in the general style of the White House,—many of them larger and much more costly,—is there any that, in point of architecture, surpasses it?' 'No; there is not one in the same class with it,' he replied deliberately."[17] For McKim the White House represented a high architectural standard from which the United States had fallen and which he worked to reattain.

McKim's "restoration" interpreted what he felt was the appropriate American image. As an accurate replication of the White House at any point in history his work was open to criticism, and it was attacked both then and subsequently as being more a new design than a restoration. McKim and his supporters (Roosevelt, Charles Moore, Glenn Brown, and Montgomery Schuyler, among others) were defensive on this issue, always using the term *restoration,* to the great infuriation of their opponents.[18] Schuyler, the architecture critic and member of the *New York Times* editorial board, described McKim's approach as a "restoration, a return to the original scheme of the White House." He rationalized: "It is at least what the original architect might have supposed to have done, if he had modern means to work with, and the modern purposes of the house to fulfill."[19] Certainly not a restoration, at least by the standards of the late twentieth century, McKim's work reinterpreted the most important house in America as the embodiment of high classicism.

Classicism as the great expression of Western civilization and the simplicity embodied in McKim's interior treatment had recently been restated by Edith Wharton and Ogden Codman in *The Decoration of Houses.* The Wharton-Codman argument owed a large debt to McKim, for his work had provided the clearest example of the new classicism and the simplified

interior. Additionally, Wharton had submitted to McKim's review portions of the manuscript, which he supported enthusiastically in a letter to Wharton: "The designer of a room should not be too slavish, whether in the composition of a building or a room, in his adherence to the letter of tradition. By conscientious study of the best examples of classic periods, including those of antiquity, it is possible to conceive a perfect result suggestive of a particular period . . . but inspired by the study of them all."[20] Wharton played a minor but a critical role in the White House remodeling, providing support through Mrs. Roosevelt for McKim's operations.

The standards that the White House came to embody can be seen in an examination of several aspects of the interior remodeling. On one hand McKim rationalized the interior, making it a series of large ceremonial spaces with a clear processional path through it. Visitors now entered by the East Wing, passing through the groin-vaulted basement (which McKim greatly admired, sensing its Roman origins, no doubt) and up a broad flight of stairs to the main floor and across the Entrance Hall. He relocated the grand staircase from the second floor, both so the State Dining Room could be expanded to seat one hundred (and the guests didn't have to sit in the hall) and to provide a more impressive entrance for the chief executive. Instead of an open wooden staircase, the president now emerged from a marble *scala regia*. From a dowdy and neighborly interior, the main floor of the White House became ceremonial.

Interior decor for the various rooms had their origin in either English or French neoclassical idioms, which were then given particularly American

---

Facing page: The State Dining Room as redesigned in 1902 by McKim, with walls richly carved and paneled in oak provided by the New York firm of Herter Brothers and Corinthian pilasters waxed to a mellow dark brown. Completing the great-hall theme, stuffed animal heads mounted high on the walls encircled the room, most of them purchased from the Hart Decorating Company in New York. According to contemporary period notions, this room suggested a dining hall in a great English country house.

interpretations through details. Both the success and some of the inherent problems can be seen in the State Dining Room, which was designed in a Georgian idiom and intended to resemble a great dining hall at an English country house. Herter Brothers provided the oak paneling stained dark and then heavily waxed so it would glow in candlelight. Corinthian pilasters articulated the walls, the frieze recalled the much admired carving of Grinling Gibbons, and the ceiling was molded plaster and resembled those shown in *Vitruvius Britannicus*. Although Flemish tapestries dating to the sixteenth or seventeenth century illustrating the *Eclogues* of Virgil hung on the walls, they spoke to the persistent pastoral and agrarian myth of the United States. Two smaller fireplaces were replaced by one large fireplace of carved white marble with lions' heads. The lions symbolized courage and strength, but to Theodore Roosevelt—in his anglophobic mood—they seemed too British. Secretary of War Elihu Root tried to assuage his fears: "Oh, those are Roman lions, not British; and anyway, all you have to do is to tell McKim to turn the corners of their mouths down." The president remained unconvinced, and after McKim's death he commissioned the animal sculptor Phemister Proctor to replace the lions with buffalo heads.[21] Around the room McKim proposed hanging twelve game heads: a buffalo, two bears (a grizzly and a Kodiak), a moose, an elk, an antelope, a white-tailed buck, a black-tailed sheep, a white-tailed sheep, a brown sheep, and two caribou.[22] Certainly intended as a compliment to Roosevelt's well-known hunting prowess, the president found that some of the heads were "an absurdity" not appropriately regal, and he ordered "really first-class" replacements.[23]

A. H. Davenport of Boston provided the furniture for the State Dining Room, which consisted of copies of Georgian dining tables, side and serving tables with marble tops and supported by federal-derived carved wooden eagles, upholstered side chairs with cabriole legs, and copies of William and Mary armchairs. The lighting fixtures, by Edward F. Caldwell & Company of New York, were silver-plated sconces and sterling silver copies of English models that were electrified. In comparison with the earlier dining room,

McKim's remodeling made the room timeless; individual elements such as the animal heads could be removed—and they were—but the remaining decor signified that this was a noble space appropriate to great events.

Among the other changes McKim made, perhaps none sums up so well his intentions as the Entrance Hall (also known as the vestibule). Here McKim removed the Tiffany glass screen installed during Chester Arthur's presidency and also the highly colored wall decorations (in Charles Moore's terms, "original and ingenious designs, as ephemeral as fashion-plates").[24] He installed a Roman Doric order with prominent mutules copied from Vignola, consisting of six paired columns, pilasters, and an entablature that provided spatial articulation. McKim ordered the room painted white with a slight buff and yellow tint.[25] Against the side walls McKim intended to hang portraits of Roosevelt and McKinley, and then in front of the tall pier mirrors would stand reproductions of Houdon's Washington and Saint-Gaudens's standing Lincoln. As a temporary measure, since these statues were not available, McKim placed plaster casts of Socrates and a Roman orator. After the restoration was completed but before the Houdon and Saint-Gaudens statues could be installed, the Roosevelts apparently had second thoughts, for Edith wrote to McKim that she and Teddy worried about how the statues might appear. They were concerned that they might be seen as part of the receiving line, "stand[ing] there in plaster loneliness after Congress had departed."[26]

The new White House represented a major shift in American aesthetics at the turn of the century. It also represented in its iconography a new nationalism, one more imperial, more obviously connected to European-based classicism. In a sense it was more chilly, as some visitors remarked, but that was part of McKim and Roosevelt's joint intention: it should impress the visitor as the residence of a leader, a house of power that ranked with the great palaces of past world powers. It gave a new definition of what would be the future of the presidency in the twentieth century and of the increased role the United States would play on the international stage.

McKIM'S RENOVATIONS

1. Edith Wharton and Ogden Codman, *The Decoration of Houses* (New York: Scribner's, 1897), 128. Information on the 1899 decoration can be found in William Seale, *The President's House* (Washington: White House Historical Association, 1986), 2:639.

2. Personal communication, Richard Slavin, Archivist, Schumacher & Co., August 19, 1992. It is unclear whether Schumacher provided the design or it came from the architects. Also, the Schumacher records indicate that Stanford White may have had a hand in the fabric selection. This lampas design was used as a wall covering in the 1952 remodeling.

3. Charles Moore, "The Restoration of the White House," *Century* 65 (April 1903): 825.

4. McKim to Olmsted, Jr., February 16, 1903, McKim, Mead & White Collection, box misc M-7, New-York Historical Society.

5. McKim's work became the subject of attack by the opposing Democratic party, and many of the articles written praising the renovations, especially those by Montgomery Schuyler (see note 18 below), were partially in response; see "Dislike New White House," *New York Times,* February 15, 1903, 8; "The New White House," February 17, 1903, 8; and "Sale of White House Relics Is Denounced," March 1, 1903, 1. In addition to Schuyler's and Glenn Brown's articles (notes 15 and 18 below), other positive reviews of McKim's work include Major J. J. Dickinson, "The New White House," *Munsey's Magazine* 29 (April 1903): 65–72; "The New White House," *Harper's Weekly* 46 (November 22, 1902): 1734; and "The Restored White House," *Harper's Weekly* 47 (April 11, 1903): 611; A. Burnely Bibb, "The Restoration of the White House," *House & Garden* 3 (March 1903): 127–39; Abby G. Baker, "The White House of the Twentieth Century," *Independent* (October 22, 1903): 2497–2507; and Esther Singleton, "The Story of the White House," in *The Story of the White House* (New York: McClure, 1907), vol. 2, chap. 28.

6. William Seale, *The White House: The History of an American Idea* (Washington: American Institute of Architects Press, 1992); *The Restoration of the White House,* Senate document 197, 57th Cong., 2d sess. (Washington: Government Printing Office, 1903).

7. Arthur M. Schlesinger, Jr., *The Imperial Presidency* (Boston: Houghton Mifflin, 1973).

8. Seale, *President's House* 2:654.

RICHARD GUY WILSON

9. Richard Guy Wilson, Dianne Pilgrim, and Richard Murray, *The American Renaissance, 1876–1917* (Brooklyn: Brooklyn Museum, 1979).

10. Quoted in Charles Moore, *Daniel H. Burnham: Architect, Planner of Cities* (Boston: Houghton Mifflin, 1921), 1:47.

11. Bernard Berenson, *The Venetian Painters* (1894), reprinted in *The Italian Painters of the Renaissance* (Cleveland: Meridian Books, 1957), iii.

12. Quoted in Robert Kerr, Supplement to James Fergusson, *History of the Modern Styles of Architecture,* 3d ed. (London, 1891), 373.

13. McKim quoted by H. Siddons Mowbray in Charles Moore, *The Life and Times of Charles Follen McKim* (Boston: Houghton Mifflin, 1929), 260.

14. Ibid., 201.

15. Nathan Miller, *Theodore Roosevelt: A Life* (New York: Morrow, 1992), 214, 324, 416–17, 426–27, 430; Samuel Eliot Morison, *The Oxford History of the American People* (New York: Oxford, 1965), 816; Glenn Brown, "Roosevelt and the Fine Arts," *American Architect* 116 (December 10, 17, 1919): 711–19, 739–52; Irving Pond, "Roosevelt and the Fine Arts," *American Architect* 116 (December 17, 1919): 723–24; and Glenn Brown, *Memories: A Winning Crusade to Revive George Washington's Vision of a Capital City* (Washington: W. H. Roberts, 1931), 141–77.

16. Colonel Theodore A. Bingham, "The Future of the White House," *Ladies Home Journal* 17 (November 1900): 9–10.

17. Moore, "Restoration of the White House," 809–11.

18. Glenn Brown, a Washington, D.C., architect, was an influential voice in Washington design issues during the turn of the century. A close friend of McKim, he assisted on Washington commissions and wrote extensively on the district and its buildings. See in particular Glenn Brown, "A Protest and Recommendation," *American Architect and Building News* 71 (January 5, 1901): 6; [Brown], "Washington: The Restoration of the White House," *American Architect and Building News* 79 (February 28, 1903): 67–70; and Brown, "The New White House," *Harper's Weekly* 50 (July 14, 1906): 989–93, 1003; Brown, *Memories,* 103–39; and Brown, "Personal Reminiscences of Charles Follen McKim," *Architectural Record* 39 (January 1916): 84–88. Schuyler wrote a number of pieces defending the White House: see Montgomery Schuyler, "The New White House in Washington, D.C.," *Architectural Record* 13 (April 1903): 359–88; unsigned editorial, "The New White House," *New York Times,* February 17, 1903, 8; "New White House: A Restoration of the Original Plan," *New York Times,* October 5, 1902, 25.

19. Schuyler, "The New White House in Washington, D.C.," 381.

20. Charles McKim, "Memoranda" "To Mrs. Wharton," ca. February 5, 1897,

in McKim Collection, Library of Congress. See also Richard Guy Wilson, "Edith and Ogden: Writing, Decoration and Architecture," in *Ogden Codman and the Decoration of Houses,* ed. Pauline Metcalf (Boston: Godine, 1988), 133–84.

21. Quoted in Moore, *McKim,* 221; see also Brown, *Memories,* 159–60. Brown recounts a letter by Roosevelt from December 7, 1919, in which the ex-president argues for using the bison with "its shaggy frontlet and mane and short curved horns" as an American symbol on buildings instead of the usual European-derived lions; he points specifically to the New York Public Library, where the "preposterous lions, [are] apparently in the preliminary stages of epilepsy" (174).

22. Blueprint of State Dining Room, 7-30-02, McKim, Mead & White Collection, New-York Historical Society.

23. George B. Cortelyou to McKim, December 1, 1902, Walker O. Cain Office.

24. Moore, *Century,* 829.

25. Glenn Brown, "The Restoration of the White House," *American Architect* 79 (1903), 70.

26. Edith K. Roosevelt to McKim, n.d. (ca. 1903), Cain Office.

NINE

Serving Those Who Serve: White House Workers

MARJORIE A. HUNT

F OR NEARLY two centuries, since the time of John Adams, the White House has been the home of American presidents. A powerful symbol of the nation, it is a uniquely private and public place—at once a family residence, a seat of the government, a ceremonial center, and a historic building and museum.

Over the years, hundreds of people have worked behind the scenes to help run the White House, preparing family meals, serving elaborate state dinners, polishing floors, tending the grounds, welcoming visitors. Today, a household staff of approximately ninety full-time domestic and maintenance employees—including butlers, maids, engineers, housemen, chefs, electricians, florists, ushers, doormen, carpenters, and plumbers—work together under one roof to operate, maintain, and preserve the 132-room Executive Mansion. These workers carry forward a long tradition of service to the nation. They bring to their jobs special skills and working knowledge accumulated over years of experience.

In commemoration of the two hundredth anniversary of the White

House, the Smithsonian Institution's Center for Folklife Programs and Cultural Studies conducted an oral history project with former White House workers, exploring the occupational culture—the techniques, customs, skills, and stories—of a wide range of White House employees and examining the distinctive ways in which the White House, as a unique occupational setting, shapes work experience.[1]

The living memory and firsthand experiences of the forty workers interviewed for the project span almost a century—sixteen presidential administrations—from the presidency of William Taft to that of Bill Clinton. Several have worked at the White House for more than thirty years, serving as many as ten first families. Lillian Parks, a 97-year-old former maid and seamstress, started working for President Hoover in 1929 and served through the Eisenhower administration; her memory of the White House goes back to 1909, when her mother, Maggie Rogers, joined the staff as a maid for President Taft. "I was twelve years old when I first started going to the White House with my mother," she says, "and I've been in and out of the White House ever since."

The oral histories and personal experiences of these workers offer valuable insights into how larger patterns of social change in the nation affected employees' daily routines and work relationships. Preston Bruce, a sharecropper's son from South Carolina who worked as a doorman for twenty-two years, tells of the thrill he felt to witness the struggle for civil rights personally from inside the White House. Others speak of how the various approaches of first families affected their ways of serving guests, conducting social events, and interacting with staff. Alonzo Fields, a ninety-three-year-old former maître d' who joined the staff in 1931, comments eloquently on what it was like to encounter segregation in the White House and how this situation changed over his twenty-seven years of service. "They had separate dining rooms—black and white. We all worked together, but we couldn't eat together. . . . Here in the White House, I'm working for the president. This is the home of *the* democracy of the world, and I'm good enough to

Emmett and Maggie Rogers pose with their daughter, Lillian, ca. 1897. Lillian Parks's mother, Maggie Rogers, worked as a White House maid for thirty years from the Taft through the Roosevelt administrations. Lillian Parks started working for President Hoover in 1929 and served through the Eisenhower administration.

Lillian Rogers Parks, a former maid and seamstress who began accompanying her mother to the White House in 1909, during the administration of William Howard Taft, seated in her home surrounded by mementos from her thirty years of work in the White House.

MARJORIE A. HUNT

handle the president's food—to handle the president's food and do everything—but I cannot eat with the help." Mr. Fields also tells of the integral role that he and a doorman, Arthur Jackson, played in gaining an eight-hour workday and compensatory time for White House workers during the Roosevelt administration:

We talked to them [the Roosevelts] about it and we carried on campaigns undercover, you know. But it didn't work. So Arthur and I came up with a solution. We started a rumor. He'd go to someone in the kitchen, someone who was very talkative, and say to him, "Have you heard of organizing, did anyone say anything to you about organizing the White House?" And they'd say no. And that person would go to someone else, and in no time it was back to the housekeeper. So the housekeeper calls me in, she says, "What's this about John L. Lewis, the CIO's gonna organize the help in the White House?" I says, "I don't know anything about it. You know they wouldn't come to me." And so then Mrs. Roosevelt and she talked it over. And Mrs. Roosevelt asked me to come up to talk to her. She says, "Do you have any way of finding out?" I says, "Well, perhaps I could get the doorman, Arthur, to find out for us." . . . So he went to the meeting and he came back and told us that they would organize us if seventy-five percent of the people would sign up. So I told her that news and when I told her that, she says, "Well that mustn't happen. Tell me, what do they want?" I says, "Well, they'd like eight hours a day and compensatory time off when they work overtime. They want pay for it." So she said she and the president didn't think it should go on the Hill. And so everybody then got eight hours a day. And so to this day, this is the first time I've told in public. That's how we got back our time and the hour.

All the employees describe working at the White House as a unique experience where work, with its variety of staged events and backstage support for them, has a strong performative element. Butlers, doormen, and chefs, for example, talk about how their employment is different from that in a luxury hotel or the household of a wealthy family, citing everything from security concerns to the high standards demanded by the realization that one's performance reflects on the president and the nation. "This is the president's house. You are serving the world, entertaining the world. It's got to be right," said Alonzo Fields. "You're working for the highest office in the land," said the doorman Preston Bruce. "You know that whatever you do is going to affect the family upstairs." To work at the White House is to serve as a guardian of the national honor. This ethos informed work performances and behavior at every level.

While first families are only temporary residents at the White House,

Housekeeper Shirley Bender inspects a guest room in the White House.

members of the household staff are permanent employees. Many have been there for more than thirty years. For these workers, the transition from one administration to the next is a difficult and challenging time. "When the different families come in, it's like sudden death. It really is like sudden death," said Alonzo Fields. "You've been with a family for eight, four, or twelve years or something like that and you have a new family coming in. You have all kinds of rumors about the incoming family. When they come to the White House the servants will know quite a bit about them. In fact, I made it my business to even go out and get books, read about them—their religion, what part of the country they come from, their viewpoints. And you would apply that."

"When the old family goes out, you felt lost for just that flash. And then at twelve o'clock when the other family comes in, you took on a new perspective. You just had to turn over; you had to forget those folks and start over," noted Lillian Parks. On Inauguration Day, workers must say farewell to a family they have served for years and begin adjusting to new ways of doing and acting, new likes and dislikes, new routines of work. "You had to adapt. That's the thing that paramount," said Mr. Fields, who experienced the dramatic shift in the White House from the formal elegance of the Hoovers to the exuberant informality of the Roosevelt family.

The Hoovers were very formal. There was an eight-course or seven-course dinner every night, even if it was only the president and Mrs. Hoover at the table. . . . So when the Roosevelts came in, the Inaugural dinner set us off. We didn't realize that this was a sudden change, a sudden change—like a storm coming in. We had a horseshoe table for seventy-five people and the menu was this: The first course was oyster stew, that wasn't bad. But the next thing was scrambled eggs, bacon and sausages, fried potatoes, and we had biscuits and hot rolls and creamed chicken and creamed peas. Now, we didn't know how to serve that. Would we serve it separately or would we put all the chicken and all on the same plate? Everybody hesitated to ask Mrs. Roosevelt, so they dared me to go over. So I politely went over and bowed to Mrs. Roosevelt and asked her about the service. Did she want all of it on the same plate? She laughed at me. She says, "Well, of course, all on the same plate." And we had hot biscuits and jam all up and down the table. Whoever served hot biscuits and jam at a formal dinner? And when we completed, the butlers asked me, "What are we gonna do?" I said, "We'll just have to change our mode and follow, follow the crowd. These people are gonna throw old man protocol right out the door." So the Roosevelts changed and we lived through that Roosevelt change for twelve years.

Another maître d', Eugene Allen, who served first eight families from the Truman through the Reagan administrations, had similar experiences:

I've seen the time that certain things we done in one administration and boy, they thought it was wrong, we should never do it. Then another administration would come in and it was perfectly all right. . . . Well, say, for the Eisenhower administration: When we had state dinners, or any dinner, Mrs. Eisenhower forbid us to pick up plates until everybody was through eating. And she would sit there and look, and if we did, she would tell us about it. And so we learned and we decided that we would not pick up a plate until everybody had eaten. So then the next administration comes in and sometimes they would want to rush things. I can recall once that President Johnson told me, he says, "Why don't you pick up?" I said, "Mr. President, your guests haven't finished eating." And he said, "Well, if you'd start picking up, they'd rush to get through!" That was just one of the little things that from one administration to the other, the differences, that one liked and the other one didn't.

MARJORIE A. HUNT

White House workers get together for a party during the Truman years.

Workers not only had to learn new routines but had to build new relationships as well. "You must earn their trust," said Mr. Fields.

When a new president goes in there, he doesn't know his way around, and he's watching you. And you must assure him—you must assure him by body language—that you have no interest other than in him, in the presidency. You don't care who's president— you're working for the public. You're a servant to the public, just like he is.

SERVING THOSE WHO SERVE

Workmen hang doors and move furniture as the 1950 renovation of the White House nears completion.

Each job at the White House—butler, carpenter, calligrapher, or cook—has a unique set of challenges, skills, tasks, and responsibilities. Workers take pride in their abilities: the mastery of special techniques, the knowledge of work processes, the exercise of proper decorum. For a butler, serving a state dinner requires not only precise timing and efficiency but also the ability to conduct oneself with social grace. "It's the presentation," said the butler Norwood Williams. Doormen take pride in the way they treat people, prizing their ability to remember names and make White House guests feel comfortable. "I had my *own* style of receiving guests," said Preston Bruce. "I remembered everybody. I greeted all the guests when they came to a state dinner. If a person came more than one time, I didn't have to ask his name." Alonzo Fields likened conducting a state dinner to conducting a symphony:

> When a dinner table was set and the president and his guests were seated at the table, I stood behind the president's chair and would give a nod to the butlers in the dining room and then everyone would move forward and serve. And with that action I pictured myself as being in charge of my orchestra. I was playing a big symphony. I had my winds and my strings and my reeds and my percussions in the back. And I was directing the biggest symphony playing any overture that made me happy. I enjoyed being at the White House.

Workers speak of efforts to devise innovative systems for accomplishing tasks and the satisfaction of adding their own personal touch to the performance of their jobs. Preston Bruce, for example, perceived a need for a more efficient way to hand out escort cards to guests coming to formal events at the White House. Working together with the carpenter Bonner Arrington, he designed a special table of the right height and width to hold all the cards. Nearly twenty years later it is still known as "Bruce's table." Alonzo Fields tells of the challenge he faced trying to figure out how to produce "double-header" teas for Mrs. Roosevelt:

> Mrs. Roosevelt, she had teas—five or six hundred a tea, twice in the same afternoon. There'd be a tea for five hundred at four o'clock and a tea for five hundred at five o'clock. Now, you've got to serve those people and get them out of there. And there's no one there to tell you how to do it. So one time I spoke to Mrs. Roosevelt. I said,

"Madam, how do you want this tea served?" She says, "Oh, I don't know. I've been told it can't be done. But that's what I want." . . . Now, I had traveled. I had played in bands. I had played in circus bands, and I had seen the tents and the rings torn down within five seconds and a new group come on in that same ring. . . . And I said, "I'll just produce this like I would a three-ring circus!" And that's what I did.

For everyone at the White House, qualities of discretion and loyalty, the ability to adapt to the different styles of successive first families, and a willingness to perform multiple duties were key work skills. "Hear nothing, know nothing, see nothing, and keep everything to yourself! That's the best quality of a good butler," said Alonzo Fields. "You've got to be flexible," said Eugene Allen. "You cannot get set in your ways, because *your* way is

Doorman Preston Bruce welcomes guests to a state dinner.

MARJORIE A. HUNT

not the way it works!" "You don't ever tell a new First Lady what the outgoing First Lady did!" noted Lillian Parks. "You let them ask *you* questions."

At the White House, a spirit of mutual support and teamwork pervades the workplace. Employees from many different units join together on a regular basis to help each other prepare for special events or accomplish tasks in daily work routines. A prime example of this cooperative spirit is a state dinner, which requires the coordinated efforts of chefs, doormen, butlers, florists, carpenters, ushers, and many others. "Everyone works like a team," said Norwood Williams, a part-time butler. "You have a crew that comes in and moves furniture and sets up tables. You have the cleaning staff, the storeroom person, the chefs, the flower shop. Even the carpenters' shop—they had to make some of those tables. You know how everyone pitches in at a circus? That's the way it's done."

Workers share stories of how their collective solidarity and diverse responsibilities have led to mutual help as part of an occupational community. "You helped the other person. Everybody, everybody knew what to do," said Lillian Parks. The plumber Howard Arrington, for example, proudly tells of how he was able to assist a pastry chef by using his metalworking skills to craft an elaborate structure to support Tricia Nixon's wedding cake. "Most of your plumbing is always hidden, but this time it showed up a little bit," he said.

Lillian Parks recounted an experience with a related set of themes:

I never knew from one day to the next what I'd be doing. One time, a fellow on the first floor said, "We need you downstairs to sew a drapery in the Green Parlor." Well, I picked up my needle and thread and I went down there. So they had this eleven-foot ladder in there, and the drapery in the Green Room—way up at the top—was coming off. Now, I went up the ladder—two steps from the top—and all I had was this needle and thread to hold me up there. And the housekeeper looked in there, and she said, "*This* I don't want to see!" And she left. And Washington, the fellow who was holding the ladder, he had a coughing spell! He started to cough and he had to walk away. . . . So you wonder why I'm still living!

In recollections by the household staff, themes of home, family, and tradition run strong. Employees often speak of themselves as a family and of the White House as a second home. Many of the workers are related and have held jobs passed down through generations. "It was just like a big family, a real big family," said Lillian Parks. "People had their differences, but they were just so kind to each other." As a close-knit occupational community, workers share skills, customs, and traditions that grow out of common experience and that are shaped by the unique demands, pressures, and conditions of the workplace. They tell stories with job-related themes: about how they came to work at the White House, their first day on the job, their greatest challenges, funny incidents, memorable characters, and relationships with famous guests and first families. Eugene Allen, for example, related a story—a cautionary tale of sorts—about a funny incident that happened to a houseman, George Thomas.

President Truman used to come over for lunch and he used to go into the Oval Room on the second floor and do some work at a desk in there. So when he'd leave and go back to the office, we had a houseman named George Thomas, and he would go in and look around and make sure the place was tidied up. So George looked around and, of course, President Truman was neat and everything was in order. So George decided that he would sit down. So he got in the president's chair—he had one of these big leather chairs, you know—and sat down. And who comes in the door but President Truman. He looked at George—he had forgot something, you know—he looked at him and said, "George, I'll tell you one thing, you're in a mighty hot seat!" He picked up his papers and went on back to the office. That was the end of that.

MARJORIE A. HUNT

Maître d' Alonzo Fields and his staff of butlers, including John Ficklin, John Pye, and Armstead Barnett, stand ready to serve a tea during the administration of Franklin Delano Roosevelt.

Howard Arrington told another tale about a worker's encounter with a president:

I remember a little story about President Johnson. He never liked to see lights left on, especially in the daytime when no one was around working. So he came into the carpentry shop one day and the lights were on and he didn't see anyone working. Well, just behind this partition one of the carpenters was framing some pictures. He had a special little framing place where he would do all the framing of the pictures for the White House. So the president reached up and flicked the lights off. This carpenter's name was Avery. Avery had a little switch in his compartment, so he switched them back on. So the president looked and he switched them back off. So Avery says, "Who in the devil is messing with those lights?" I think that's the way the words were, might have been a little stronger. But anyway, the president switched them back off and that time Avery was hot, so Avery stepped outside and he came nose to nose with the president and the president told him *he* was the one that was cutting the lights off. And Avery was so taken by shock that all he could think of and do was just stand up and salute the president, and that's all he did!

"There were so many funny things that happened," said Lillian Parks, recounting a story about another houseman at the White House, named Herman Thompson:

> He was always answering phones, talking on the phone. So one day he answered and someone said, "I'd like to order lunch for Mrs. Wallace and me." And Herman said, "Who is 'me'?" And the voice said, "I happen to be the president of the United States." After that, all the guys were teasing and joking with him: "Better clean out your locker, Herman. You're outta here!"

Many of the workers' stories have been handed down through the generations from one group of workers to the next. Alonzo Fields recounts a story about President Taft that dates to the early 1900s:

> There's a story about President Taft. He was a great, great eater, as you know. And he wouldn't drink champagne in a champagne glass, he had a water goblet of champagne. And he would go to sleep at the table after dinner and they'd have to stay there with him. One man, Samuel Jackson, Mr. Barnett's uncle, he was with him and he'd stay there sometimes till one-thirty in the morning, unless Mrs. Taft would come down and get him. You didn't have air conditioning in those days, and on Sundays they'd have lunch under the old magnolia tree. So it seems that the president had had his champagne and big meal and he went to sleep under that old tree. And so the presi-

Chef Henry Haller prepares a dinner in the White House kitchen.

dent would huff and puff, and he'd puff and puff and saw, and then he would huff and puff until a little bird up in the tree became disturbed and he bombed away with keen precision and hit the president's mustache. Jackson was there with him as usual and Jackson ran over as the president exploded, so Jackson tells me, and he went over and he cleaned the president's mustache up, and he said, "Jackson, if you ever tell this I'll have your head on a platter!"

Perhaps one of the most memorable characters of the White House—and the subject of a whole cycle of tales—is Charlie Thompson, a messenger who started work back in the bicycle days for President Coolidge and served up to the Eisenhower administration, retiring when he was in his eighties.

Rex Scouten, curator of the White House, related a story about one of Charlie's misadventures:

Charlie Thompson was a messenger at the White House. I remember he started there as a messenger on bicycle delivering paychecks on Capitol Hill and around town. I know he was at the White House at least since the Coolidge administration, maybe earlier than that. Well, when I knew him he was a messenger whose primary job was delivering newspapers. So every time he came by—I was in the Secret Service at that time—and Charlie would walk by and always hold out the newspapers and you could see the headlines. So one day I was outside the Cabinet Room and they were having a cabinet meeting. So Charlie came by and as he's walking down the hall, he showed the headline and he spun around and he made one extra quarter turn and walked right into the Cabinet Room! He took one step in and shot back out of there and out the door and down the colonnade! By that time, the other door opened, and I can't remember exactly who it was, but I think it was the cabinet secretary, and he said, "Who the hell was that?" And I said, "Well, it's only Charlie Thompson, he's been around here for a long, long time." "I guess he's been around here too damn long!"

As an occupational community, workers also share nicknaming traditions and take part in employee customs like the annual Christmas party, the golf tournament, and staff reunions. "We had a lot of fun with nicknames," said Lillian Parks. "Melvin Carter, he was small and everybody used to call him 'Squirt.' I was 'Maggie's Little Girl' or 'Mama.' And Traphes was 'Paddlefoot' because he walked right flat-footed." "We had code names for the presidents," writes Alonzo Fields in his published memoirs. "President Hoover, because he seldom smiled, we called 'Smiley.' President Roosevelt I gave the name 'Charlie Potatoes.' . . . President Truman, because of his outspoken manner, we coded as 'Billie Spunk.'"[2] Mr. Fields himself was nicknamed "Donald Duck" by the butlers who worked for him because of the way he sputtered and yelled when something went wrong. "We had a good time," said Lillian Parks. "People would say some of the funniest things, make you die. And *do* some funny things. There was never a dull day."

At the White House, knowledge of work techniques and routines, traditions of service and decorum, and other codes of behavior are passed down through word of mouth and by imitation and example. Experienced old-timers teach new generations of workers by telling stories and jokes, sharing personal experience, and demonstrating work methods. Samuel Ficklin, a part-time butler at the White House for half a century, from the Roosevelt to the Bush administrations, tells of the training he received from his brother, Charles, and Alonzo Fields when he first started:

> They made sure that I was ready to go out to be a butler. My brother, Charles, told me, he said, "In order for you to be a good butler, take some bricks, put one in each hand and strengthen your muscles that way, so that you'll be able to hold a heavy tray without shaking and let someone be served from it." And Mr. Fields was very strict, especially when we were setting the table. He showed where that plate is supposed to be and you measured with your thumb. You put it up against the table and there goes that plate and then that's right. And then everything would be uniform. I give him all the credit.

Norwood Williams tells of the lessons he learned on his first day on the job as a butler:

> The first thing I did was to go to the White House and be met by Mr. Fields and Mr. Crim. And Mr. Fields took me in to meet President Truman. And he said, "Mr. President, we have a new butler here today and I would like to introduce you to Mr. Norwood

Maître d' Alonzo Fields greets President and Mrs. Harry S Truman.

MARJORIE A. HUNT

Williams." And the president says, "How would you like to be called? Would you like to be called Norwood or Williams?" I said, "It's a pleasure to meet you, Mr. Truman." And Alonzo had spasms because you don't call the president of the United States Mr. Truman. He never said a mumbling word, but his fists got real red and he was holding them down at his side and I looked over at him. Alonzo Fields, I'll tell you, was a stickler for excellence. I didn't have that. I was young. But I got that discipline from him.

A critical body of accumulated knowledge and wisdom resides in these workers, who over decades of change—as first families come and go—remain a key source of continuity at the White House. Acknowledged authorities on everything from where tea napkins are stored to how to welcome visiting dignitaries, they provide a valuable link between past and present. "When a new administration comes in they're just as in the dark as anybody else—they don't know what to do. So as butlers, we have been there. We can kind of carry them along; we can help them along," said John Johnson, a butler at the White House for thirty years. And Lillian Parks related, "After I retired, the usher called me and said, 'Lillian, I wish you'd come down here and straighten this house out!' It was all kind of mixed up. . . . You see, I grew up in there. I knew how things worked." Through traditions of teaching and learning, a culture of White House work is established, maintained, and adapted.

White House workers embody social and cultural history. Their memories and stories help us to understand the White House in human terms—as a home and a workplace, a public building and a national symbol. Their perspective, shaped by years of personal experience, adds a rich dimension to the historical record.

For all of these employees, to work at the White House was to be at the heart of the nation. Many were honored to be serving their country, excited to be a part of history in the making, proud to be carrying forward traditions of service and social ceremony passed down over two centuries.

SERVING THOSE WHO SERVE

The White House residence staff poses in the State Dining Room, ca. 1982.

"I didn't feel like a servant to a man," said Mr. Fields. "I felt I was a servant to my government, to my country." The White House, as both a workplace and a symbol, affected them deeply and shaped their working lives. In turn, these workers left a lasting mark on the White House. Their dedication, pride, and skill remain in the techniques they devised, the traditions they preserved, and the knowledge they passed down to others. Their artistry and care continue to affect the way that things are done, preserving a rich legacy for generations to come.

MARJORIE A. HUNT

NOTES

1. The "Workers at the White House" oral history collection is housed in the Archives of the Smithsonian Institution's Center for Folklife Programs and Cultural Studies. Unless otherwise noted, all quotations in this essay are drawn from this oral history collection.

2. Alonzo Fields, *My 21 Years in the White House* (New York: Coward-McCann, 1960), 184.

Caring for the White House Today

GARY WALTERS

MOST PEOPLE are aware that the White House is unique in its historical significance, unique in its symbolism and link with American democracy, and unique in its bond to the American people. The preceding essays have attempted to take the measure of the White House's role in American history. The present epilogue, in contrast, attempts to answer a nonhistorical question about the Executive Residence at the White House, as it is officially known today, namely, How do we care for the White House today?

The immediate response is, Very carefully—a lot of people are watching! I recently received a verbal reproach from a woman who works for a local tour operation that frequently brings bus tour groups through the Executive Residence as part of the daily public tours. She complained that the mirror hung high over the fireplace mantel in the Blue Room had apparently been neglected, as the dark fingerprint smudges she had seen on an earlier visit had not yet been cleaned away. I responded that I would see the housekeeper about the problem immediately. I didn't have the heart to tell her that what she called smudges were a breakdown of the paint on this ca. 1815 reverse-painted looking glass, which had been hanging in that location and in that same condition for nearly twenty years.

This incident demonstrates the extent to which people identify with the Executive Residence; her complaint originated from genuine concern for the Residence, not solely as criticism of the housekeeping staff. The Executive Residence belongs to the American people, and they expect it to be cared for properly. The White House is the only residence of a sitting head of state or government that is open to the public on a regular basis, Tuesday through Saturday from eight in the morning until twelve noon, without any charge or fee.

To explain the care given to the Executive Residence, it is necessary to understand the relationship between the Residence and the National Park Service, the responsibilities of the Chief Usher, and the daily operation of the Executive Residence. The Executive Residence sits on just over eighteen acres of ground originally chosen as the site for the President's House by President George Washington and his city planner, Major Pierre-Charles L'Enfant. The house was to occupy a much larger parcel of land known today as President's Park, an area that is now administered by the National Park Service and encompasses LaFayette Park across Pennsylvania Avenue to the north, the grounds and gardens of the Executive Residence, and the Ellipse to the south. The Congressional Residence Act of 1790 established the new federal city "on the river Potomac." It also authorized the president to appoint three commissioners to survey and purchase land for the new city and, in 1792, to have the federal commissioners supervise the early construction of the Capitol and the President's House. Additional legislation through the years established the National Park Service and placed it in its role of preserving what is "Reservation Numbered 1 . . . known as the White House."

The relationship between the White House and the Park Service continues today. As a separate agency of the federal government, the Executive

Looking glass, gilded wood and eglomise (reverse-painted glass) panel, possibly New York, ca. 1815, in the Blue Room. It is suggestive of a mirror designed by Benjamin Henry Latrobe (an 1809 drawing survives) for the oval drawing room (the interior we know today as the Blue Room). In his decoration of the interior for President and Mrs. Madison, Latrobe placed over the mantel a giant "French plate" glass mirror, embellished with a marbleized frame and lambrequin crown and edged in gilt balls. It was destroyed in the fire of 1814.

GARY WALTERS

Residence is required to develop and transmit to the Congress, through the Office of Management and Budget, an appropriation request like all other Executive Branch agencies. In an attempt to keep the Executive Residence out of the political arena, as a home owned by the American people and lent every four years to our elected leader, the National Park Service's National Capital Regional Director presents the Residence budget to the Congress and, in fact, testifies before House and Senate committees on behalf of the Executive Residence appropriation. The National Park Service is responsible for major repairs to the Executive Residence, furnishes a maintenance staff for the grounds and gardens, and provides a storage facility for the White House Fine Arts Collection and other items used in support of all Executive Residence activities within the White House.

As Chief Usher of the White House, I am responsible for administering the Executive Residence at the White House and directing the eighty-six members of the Residence staff. My primary charge is to carry out the desires of the First Family as they relate to the three main functions of the Residence: (1) the home of the president and his family; (2) a historical site visited by almost 1.2 million visitors each year; and (3) the site of numerous official and ceremonial events of the presidency.

A former Chief Usher, J. B. West, wrote in his book, *Upstairs at the White House,* that when he was asked the now very familiar question, "What does the Chief Usher do?" his usual reply was "I do what I am told to do"—a most succinct and appropriate answer that I now use quite often. In carrying out these responsibilities, the Chief Usher must coordinate Executive Residence actions and policies with numerous other agencies, including the Executive Office of the President, the National Park Service, the Secret Service, the General Services Administration, the military, and many other government and private entities.

The highly motivated and dedicated staff of the Executive Residence, some of whom have served the presidency for more than forty-five years, are divided into four basic classifications: administration, mechanical and maintenance, domestic services, and specialized professionals. Members of the Residence staff are federal employees who serve at the pleasure of the president and are not protected by normal civil service regulations.

The administrative function is performed by the Chief Usher's immediate staff of seven, assigned to oversee daily operations of the Residence and its grounds and gardens, and to manage the accounting function for the Executive Residence. The congressional appropriation language states that funds are provided to the president "for the care, maintenance, repair, alteration, refurnishing, improvement, heating, and lighting, including electrical power and fixtures, of the Executive Residence at the White House and official entertainment expenses of the President." The Chief Usher is the president's designated officer to administer this appropriation.

The mechanical and maintenance staff of thirty-four includes operating engineers who work on a twenty-four-hour basis maintaining the forty-year-old heating, air-conditioning, and ventilating systems; electricians; plumbers; carpenters; painters; and an operations section that readies the public areas each morning and afternoon for the daily tours and prepares for the many functions that take place in the Residence and on the grounds.

The domestic force of thirty-eight includes the housekeeping staff, which is responsible for the daily cleaning of the 132 rooms of the Residence, and the kitchen staff, which orders, picks up, stores, and prepares all the food that is served for official functions (there were 166 such functions in 1991, with 34,520 guests). The chefs prepare daily meals for the president, his family, and their guests. We meticulously account for the food and beverage, down to the lemon wedges used with tea, as well as for personal items used, for which the government receives reimbursement directly from the president. The domestic staff also includes a maître d' and five butlers, who provide food and beverage service and give direction to the part-time butlers hired for larger events when additional help is required.

The specialized group of Residence staff members is a highly skilled and talented group of professionals. It includes the White House curators, who

GARY WALTERS

Stewart Stevens cleaning an East Room chandelier.

EPILOGUE

are charged with caring for the more than 33,822 items in the Executive Residence inventory, including the White House Fine Arts Collection, which has been showcased in the White House Historical Association's publication *Art in the White House: A Nation's Pride,* and providing information on the White House and its possessions; the calligraphers, who create the treasured White House invitations and other handwritten documents; and the Residence florists, who provide cut floral arrangements for the publicly viewed rooms and floral decorations for official functions, as has been the tradition of the White House from its earliest days.

A discussion of the care of the White House today must begin with a review of how the Executive Residence operates at present. For this discussion, I will define the present time as the years since 1976, a year that marked a major change in the operation of the Executive Residence. During the American bicentennial celebration, two significant occurrences fundamentally altered the way that the White House is used. First, the foreign heads of state and heads of government who visited the United States to help commemorate the bicentennial concentrated the celebration on the presidency, thereby generating more official and ceremonial events than the White House had previously seen. Second, the assassination attempts on President Ford in late 1975 caused a review of the methods and activities that surrounded presidential exposure. The logical solution for the two newly posed circumstances was to merge them. The White House and its Residence staff had shown that they could withstand the greater level of activity, and the White House was certainly an obvious choice from a security standpoint.

Now, instead of the president's going out of the White House complex to meet with and speak before various groups, the groups were brought to the relatively secure environment of the Executive Residence. This arrangement had the added benefit of saving a great deal of time and government money, as each presidential movement outside the White House gates requires immense planning and demands a good deal of the president's time.

Bringing presidential events within the White House complex has dramatically changed the level of activity within the Executive Residence. Before 1976 there were normally fewer than five or six events held in the Residence per month; now it is not unusual to have that many in just one week.

A typical day for the Residence and its staff begins at six in the morning, when the first operations personnel and part of the housekeeping staff arrive to begin the setup for the congressional tours, which start at eight o'clock. These are referred to as congressional tours because tickets must be obtained through a senator or congressperson. The housekeeping staff must ensure that everything is clean before the operations staff moves furniture and rolls up carpets to make room for the placement of heavy rubber floor runners to protect the oak flooring in the state floor parlors and the State Dining Room. Carpets on the ground floor are removed entirely to make way for the tourists, while a heavy rubber matting is placed on the mahogany floor in the China Room to protect it from the punishing foot traffic of some 1,200 ticketed tourists who will go through the first two floors of the Residence by ten o'clock, when the public tours begin. The daily cleaning of the glass entry doors is accomplished by the custodial specialist, who, among other duties, annually hand-cleans each of the more than six thousand pieces of cut glass in each of the three grand chandeliers in the East Room.

Meanwhile, the electricians are starting their daily walk-through to check for burnt-out, unplugged, or nonworking lamps and light bulbs in the 132 rooms of the residence. Our senior maintenance advisor begins his routine check of the many tall-case or grandfather clocks, antique mantel clocks, and wall banjo clocks to ensure that they maintain the correct time, while also checking for other possible maintenance problems. The carpenters check all the wood floors and buff or polish them as required. The florists refresh the floral arrangements along the tour route and provide fresh flowers to the Oval Office, while the kitchen staff and the butlers have prepared and served any morning meals. By seven o'clock the Residence staff supervisors have checked with the Usher's Office, which has been in operation since five, to get their work assignments for the day's activities—all of this before eight o'clock in the morning.

Once the daily tours have begun, the maintenance and housekeeping staffs start their routine of cleaning, polishing, and the never-ending task of preventative maintenance. The Executive Residence was rebuilt, with the exception of the exterior sandstone walls, during the Truman administration, from 1948 to 1952, at which time the house and its mechanical systems were, to use a term of today, state of the art. We are now maintaining systems that are more than forty years old and have no replacement parts.

Chefs in the White House kitchen preparing food for luncheons and afternoon and evening receptions. A typical reception might include as many as 350 guests.

GARY WALTERS

This is certainly a tribute to the operating engineers who have kept these now outdated mechanical systems in working order well beyond their normal life expectancy.

At the conclusion of the day's tours, at approximately half past twelve, the Residence staff must reverse the earlier procedures and restore the house by removing the items that were put into place earlier that morning, and get ready for any function that might be on the schedule later that afternoon or evening.

After preparing the morning meals for the president, his family, or any guests who might be visiting, the kitchen staff begins preparation of the luncheon meals and any other culinary items for functions that are occurring that afternoon or evening. A typical afternoon reception includes up to 350 guests, with food served in the State Dining Room, and guests throughout the state floor with their food and beverage carrying on conversations in the precisely placed seating arrangements of antique furniture in the parlors.

Visiting museum curators often react with disbelief when told that guests are permitted to use the antique furniture as it was originally intended. Fortunately, most of the accidental damage that has occurred has been to the upholstery, which is replaceable although expensive, but not destructive to the furniture in most cases. One case where the damage was indeed structural occurred during the occasion of the visit of Lech Walesa of Poland to the United States, in November 1989, to receive the Medal of Freedom from President Bush. After the presentation ceremony, a grand buffet was set in the State Dining Room with trays of hors d'oeuvres spread along the outside edges of the nineteenth-century mahogany table. When a butler removed one of the trays near the edge of the table and began to replace it with another full tray, a guest standing near the table saw the opening and proceeded to lift his leg and sit on the edge of the table. The table's pedestal leg broke, the table began to give way under his weight, and the trays of food began to slide toward the guest. The offender headed for the exit with the Chief Usher in close, but unfortunately not close enough, pursuit. Repair

of the table was possible, but the story remains an illustration of the struggle between daily use and curatorial protection.

Such repairs, of course, cost money. The White House is now accredited by the American Association of Museums, and no museum operates without sufficient funding. Fortunately, the Executive Residence has a large constituency—the American people—who support the preservation of the Residence and its contents through their congressional representatives. Each year, when the Executive Residence budget is presented to the congressional committees, the first question invariably asked is, What is the condition of the White House?, followed very quickly by, What are you doing for our White House tourists?

Some years ago, during Senate subcommittee hearings on the Executive Residence budget for fiscal year 1990, a discussion ensued about the desire of the White House curators to begin a comprehensive study of and conservation effort for many of the antique furnishings currently used in the state floor rooms. The conservation effort was to begin the following year, and the appropriation request was to be $100,000 per year for the next four years. The committee was so impressed by the need for the funding and the details provided in support of the conservation effort that they requested an immediate start to the project and added $125,000 to that year's budget request, thereby starting the conservation project a year early.

That is not to say that we always have the funds required to maintain the Residence and its contents properly. Each fiscal year we determine what the priorities are, within federal budget constraints and limits, and that determines the funding requested in our appropriation. There are always pressing needs. With over one million tourists and nearly forty thousand official guests in a year, the normal, everyday wear and tear on the Residence and its furnishings is enormous.

_____

Facing page: Opera star Beverly Sills sings the finale of *The Merry Widow* while dancing with President Carter at the Governor's Ball.

GARY WALTERS

Replacement of the East Room floor in 1977. Between the renovation of the White House in 1952 and 1977, some twenty-five million visitors had worn the floor down to the point where further refinishing was impossible. A million visiting tourists a year simply wear out the physical fabric of the White House in time.

Facing page: The early nineteenth-century English mahogany dining table in the State Dining Room, surrounded by Queen Anne–style chairs, displays part of Monroe's gilt service purchased from France in 1817. Carved into the marble mantel of this room is an inscription from a letter written by John Adams on his second night in the White House: "I Pray Heaven to Bestow the Best of Blessing on This House and on All that shall hereafter Inhabit it. May none but Honest and Wise Men ever rule under this Roof."

EPILOGUE

On September 22, 1961, President Kennedy signed legislation establishing "the museum character of the principal corridor on the ground floor and the principal public rooms on the first floor of the White House." On November 3, 1961, the nonprofit White House Historical Association was established to help carry out the intent of the 1961 legislation. The Historical Association, through its sales of informational materials on the White House, provides limited funding for Residence preservation projects, acquisitions of White House–related artifacts, and portraits of presidents and First Ladies. Within the last four years the association has established the White House Endowment Fund, with the goal of raising a 25-million-dollar endowment for the White House. They are just over halfway to that goal. The proceeds from the endowment will be used for White House conservation and redecoration projects, in coordination with the Chief Usher's requests.

President Johnson, following up on the work begun by President and Mrs. Kennedy, issued Executive Order 11145 on March 7, 1964, to create the Committee for the Preservation of the White House to advise the president on his responsibilities under the 1961 legislation by giving "recommendations as to the articles of furniture, fixtures, and decorative objects which shall be used or displayed . . . as to the decor and arrangements therein best suited to enhance the historic and artistic values of the White House."

The Committee comprises permanent members, including the director of the National Park Service, who acts as chairman; the Chief Usher; the White House curator; the director of the National Gallery of Art; the chairman of the Commission of Fine Arts; the secretary of the Smithsonian Institution; and any other members the president may appoint. When the public rooms require redecoration, it is the responsibility of the committee to advise the president on any possible changes that should be made to the historic character of the rooms. Currently, the committee is undertaking the redecoration of the Blue Room, which has remained basically unchanged

In 1972 the oval Blue Room was redecorated with many furnishings in the French Empire style—the decor chosen for the room by President James Monroe in 1817. The Empire style originated in France during Napoleon's reign and is characterized by richly carved rectilinear furniture based on Greek, Roman, and Egyptian forms from antiquity. A settee and seven of the original gilded chairs fashioned for Monroe by the Parisian cabinetmaker Pierre-Antoine Bellangé form the nucleus of the present furnishings.

EPILOGUE

since its last redecoration in the early 1970s. After twenty years, the drapes are faded and becoming threadbare from the effects of ultraviolet light; we have run out of fabric to recover the 1817 Bellangé furniture originally purchased by President Monroe for the room; the carpet is worn through in a number of spots and can no longer be repaired; and the wallpaper needs to be replaced. Armed with current research providing more historically correct information on furniture of the period, the committee has devised a decoration scheme for the Blue Room, including a new carpet that will be purchased with the first proceeds of the White House Endowment Fund.

Care of the White House begins with the daily activities of the Residence staff, but without the support of the president and his wife, the Congress, and the American people, nothing could be accomplished and the White House would quickly deteriorate and probably be torn down in favor of a more utilitarian structure. Having now served more than twenty-three years at the White House, I can tell you that each family for whom I have had the pleasure of serving has held the White House in utmost regard, not just as their personal residence, but as a repository of American history and culture. No other building in this country has such a profound place in the hearts of all Americans.

GARY WALTERS

ILLUSTRATION CREDITS

ABBREVIATIONS USED IN CREDITS

HABS   Historic American Buildings Survey
LC   Library of Congress
NPS   National Park Service
WH   White House
WHHA   White House Historical Association

COLOR PHOTOGRAPHS

ILLUSTRATION CREDITS

INDEX